Forms of Address

Forms of Address

A Guide for Business and Social Use

Andrea Holberg, editor

Sonia Garza
Kathleen D. Kelly
Kathleen A. Moses,
contributors

Rice University Press, Houston, Texas
in association with
the Houston International Protocol Alliance

Rice University Press
P.O. Box 1892
Houston, Texas 77251

Library of Congress Cataloging-in-Publication Data

Forms of address : a guide for business and social use / edited by
Andrea Holberg.
     p. cm.
Includes bibliographical references and index.
ISBN -0-89263-333-6 (cl.) -- ISBN 0-89263-334-4 (pa.)
1. Letter writing. 2. English language -- Address, Forms of. 3.
Commerical correspondence. 4. Etiquette. I. Holberg, Andrea,
1969--
PE1483.F67 1994
395'.52'0973--dc20   94-17521
                                                          CIP

Table of Contents

About the Houston International Protocol Alliance

The Houston International Protocol Alliance was established in 1983 as an independent, non-profit organization under contract to the City of Houston. It is funded by local hotel and motel tax revenues. The Alliance acts as the city's office of protocol and serves as the official city liaison to the resident consular corps. It provides a formal welcome to visiting foreign government dignitaries, coordinating more than 120 such visits each year. The Alliance advises the mayor, the city council, and the general public on protocol and cultural issues and administers Houston's twelve sister-city relationships.

The organization is a resource to all who come into contact with the international community. It is especially useful to the business community. The Alliance provides advice on protocol issues ranging from introductions and seating to flags and red carpets, information on cultural issues, and assistance in planning visits by foreign dignitaries. The organization also provides briefings and training materials on protocol, events planning, and intercultural matters to companies and community groups. It publishes a bimonthly newsletter, *The Envoy*, and a quarterly directory, *The Consular Corps of Houston*, both of which are available by subscription.

The Protocol Alliance is a department of the Greater Houston Convention and Visitors Bureau. Its eight-member advisory board is chaired by the mayor and comprises representatives of the city's primary international organizations. The board includes the chairs of the African American Institute of Houston, the Asia Society of Houston, the Greater Houston Convention and Visitors Bureau, the Greater Houston Partnership, the Houston Hispanic Chamber of Commerce, the Port of Houston Authority, and the Southern Region Advisory Board of the Institute of International Education. The dean of the Consular Corps of Houston is an ex-officio member.

Today, the Protocol Alliance has a staff of five working to fulfill its mission of promoting Houston in the international community.

Acknowledgments

As the office of protocol for the City of Houston, each year the Protocol Alliance answers thousands of inquiries regarding forms of address. Compiling written information seemed a logical and effective way to respond to those who contact us. Our initial efforts to organize that material eventually resulted in this full-length book, which not only presents a large amount of information, but also explores new territory and touches on a wide range of related issues.

During the development of this project, the Protocol Alliance has undergone many changes, both big and small. Several staff members who have come and gone made special contributions to the book and deserve to be acknowledged. Paige Gibson, who was office manager when we began this project, developed the initial version of the unique page layout used in our examples. This layout enabled us to present a visual representation of the required form of address and proved to be much easier to use than any list or chart. Kathleen Kelly was our executive director for several years, and as such provided a wealth of editing expertise, great ideas, and motivation. Kate Moses has the distinction of being the most detail-oriented person ever to grace the offices of the Protocol Alliance, and was exhaustive in investigating the finer points of usage. She also did a great deal of research regarding Arab culture and Islam, allowing us to include protocol information that we have never found in print. Sonia Garza did the office's basic research on forms of address when she first joined the Protocol Alliance several years ago, and since then has edited this book many times, pointing out more than a few gaps and inconsistencies. As executive director, she has worked tirelessly for its completion and publication.

Any project of this magnitude requires the work of many, many people, and we sincerely appreciate all those who have read and edited our manuscript, answered our questions on the "picky details" of usage, and most of all, encouraged us to persevere over the last three years. We would also like to thank in advance everyone who shares with us his or her experiences and all those who call our office with questions. We become aware of issues relating to forms of address by talking to people who must confront them, and we hope to include new entries and revised information based on your comments in future editions of this book.

Introduction

To judge from the many calls that the Protocol Alliance receives each day, it seems that no other issue of protocol causes greater confusion than how to address someone. Not a day passes without an enquiry regarding how to refer to a former president, how to address a letter to an ambassador, or how to properly introduce the mayor.

Their quest for answers speaks well of the Houstonians who call us, for it shows that we are all beginning to realize the importance of names and titles and their proper usage. As the number and frequency of our international contacts increases, we encounter new challenges in addressing people from different countries and cultures. Our own culture seems to place less emphasis on names and forms of address than many others. For us to relate well to the international community, we must acknowledge this. It is the right of all individuals to be addressed with respect, by using the appropriate names and forms of address.

There are several books available on the subject of business etiquette and protocol, most of which contain some general information on forms of address. This work represents a departure from the others in several ways. First, its focus is rather narrow, encompassing only the proper forms of address for titled officials. This allows us to treat the subject in greater depth. Second, the unique format of this book provides an easier way to illustrate this information. Lastly, and most importantly, this book is the product of years of research and experience gained through our work at the Houston International Protocol Alliance. Many of the issues we must handle as the city's office of protocol, such as those involving married couples with different last names and female elected officials, were nonexistent until recently. We have also found answers to questions unique to local government that are not addressed in books designed for a strictly federal audience. This book includes all levels of government, and foreign officials as well.

Introduction

As we began to research these issues, we found that the standard references do not always agree on proper forms of address. For some titles and positions, there was no information available at all. In compiling the information for this book, we have made decisions based on our own experiences. You may not always agree with our choices and you may find that sometimes it is necessary to modify the "ideal" or "most correct" form for reasons of space or convenience. We hope that this guide will serve as a basis for making an informed decision.

Although we have tried to cover as many possibilities as we could foresee, this document is by no means complete. You may encounter a title that we do not address, or a way to use a name that we have not considered. Perhaps an individual prefers a title or form of address that is not standard. In addition, titles and styles of address change over time. We hope that by using this guide as a reference tool, you will be able to make an educated decision when confronted with a new situation. For those of you who, like us, become interested in the ever-changing world of forms of address, we have included a bibliography for further study. If you are ever in doubt, we are always available to answer your questions.

Sample Entry

All of the entries in this book follow the same basic format. The style and format we consider to be most appropriate for each title are used here, but it may be necessary for you to make some small adaptations. For example, if a line contains a particularly long title or country name, it may be necessary to break it up into two lines.

Please note that the format shown for any rank (such as an ambassador or a minister) will suit all individuals of that rank, but their exact titles may differ. For example, the position of Chief of Protocol of the United States carries the rank of ambassador, and the individual may be called "Mr. Ambassador," even though the word is not a part of the job title. Thus, if you cannot find a particular title listed, but you know the individual's general rank, you may be able to formulate the correct form of address based on our entries.

Title or general rank of the official appears here.

Business Correspondence

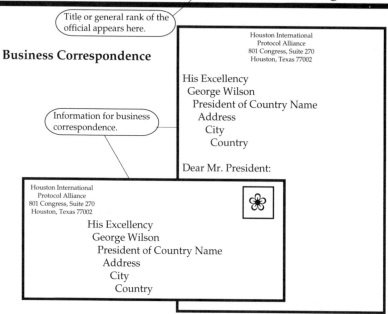

Information for business correspondence.

Houston International
Protocol Alliance
801 Congress, Suite 270
Houston, Texas 77002

His Excellency
George Wilson
President of Country Name
Address
City
Country

Dear Mr. President:

Houston International
Protocol Alliance
801 Congress, Suite 270
Houston, Texas 77002

His Excellency
George Wilson
President of Country Name
Address
City
Country

Social Correspondence

The appropriate format for personal letters or invitations.

His Excellency
The President of
Country Name*
and Mrs. Wilson
Address
City
Country

Place card

The form of address for formal place cards.

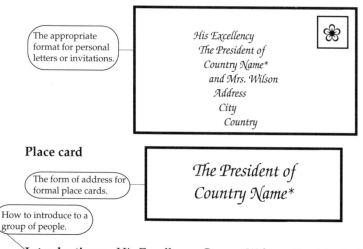

The President of
Country Name*

How to introduce to a group of people.

Introductions: His Excellency George Wilson, President of Country Name

Conversation: Your Excellency, or Mr. President

How to address in conversation or introduce to an individual.

Footnotes clarify any unusual items in each entry.

* In both of these cases, it is preferable to keep "President of Country Name" all on one line if space permits.

Business Correspondence

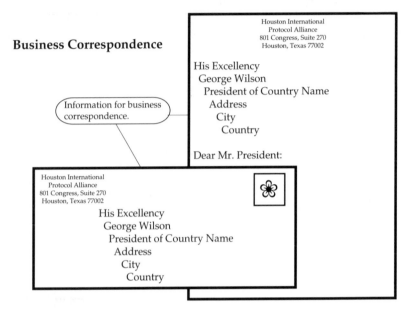

The forms of address for business correspondence are illustrated for each office. We supply the customary courtesy title, office title, and salutation for each entry. There may be individual exceptions to these suggestions, but we have used the most common titles in each case.

Indented lines are used for addresses in our examples. This format reflects a more formal style and is widely used in official and diplomatic correspondence. However, a block format is also appropriate.

Social Correspondence

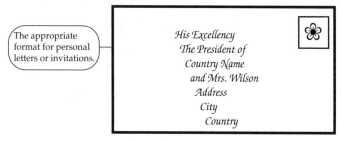

The appropriate format for personal letters or invitations.

His Excellency
The President of
Country Name
and Mrs. Wilson
Address
City
Country

The format for addressing social correspondence, invitations, and personal letters is different from that used for business correspondence.

Although typed envelopes are appropriate for business events, envelopes for social invitations should be hand addressed. Computerized calligraphy or even high-quality, laser-printed script may be substituted if necessary. Postage stamps should be used rather than metered postage, and ideally the return address should be on the back flap of the envelope. Although abbreviations are acceptable for business correspondence, in social correspondence nothing on the envelope should be abbreviated, with the exception of "Mr.," "Mrs.," and "Dr." Invitations should specify if spouses are invited, or if an unmarried individual may bring a guest.

Business addresses may be used for all business-related social events and for official social correspondence, unless the recipient is a close personal friend.

Place Cards

Place card

The form of address for formal place cards.

The President of Country Name

The Protocol Alliance answers more questions about place cards than any other subject, perhaps because most people feel more comfortable writing letters than hosting formal dinners. Luckily, there are a few general rules that can help. For the most part, the place-card format is simple: Mr. (or Mrs., or Dr., etc.) and the official's last name. For the highest-ranking dignitaries and members of royalty, the proper form for a place card is simply their title: "The President," "The Swedish Ambassador," "The Duke of Kent." If there is more than one guest of this type with the same title, such as ministers of foreign affairs for two or more countries, add their country names. For example, instead of three cards reading "The Minister of Foreign Affairs," specify "The Minister of Foreign Affairs of Denmark," "The Minister of Foreign Affairs of the Republic of France," and "The Minister of Foreign Affairs of Chile."

There are some officials whose place cards incorporate both a title and a name — "Senator Johnson" or "Mayor Brown," for example— but most will comprise either one or the other. You may occasionally need to bend the rules a little if stimulating conversation is your main goal: for example, instead of "Mr. Jones" we often prefer to use "Council Member Jones of Small Town," simply because it is more informative, if not more correct.

A spouse is generally seated in accordance with the official's rank, but no note of the spouse's position should appear on the place card. Thus, unless he or she also holds an official position (which you might like to acknowledge), each spouse's place card should read simply "Mrs. Jones" or "Mr. Scott."

If you are planning a very large event, or if there is more than one guest with the same name, it will be necessary to use full names. For example, if there are two Mrs. Smiths, one place card should read "Mrs. Jason Smith" and the other "Mrs. David Smith."

How to introduce to a group of people.

Introductions: His Excellency George Wilson, President of Country Name

Conversation: Your Excellency, or Mr. President

How to address in conversation or introduce to an individual.

Each entry in this guide includes a listing for introductions. This is the title to use when introducing the official to an audience or a large group. In normal conversation, or when introducing one person to another, we suggest using the forms found under "Conversation," as these are still respectful but more personal.

For example, if introducing an ambassador at a luncheon, you might say "Ladies and gentlemen, please welcome His Excellency John Smith, the Ambassador of the Republic of Botswana." When speaking to the ambassador personally, you would say "Mr. Ambassador, may I please present my colleague, Mary Jones? Mary, this is Ambassador Smith of Botswana." Mary might answer, "Mr. Ambassador, it's a pleasure to meet you." As you may already know, you should present a junior person to a senior one. When there is doubt as to who is senior, make introductions to the visitor as a sign of respect.

Name Tags

Name tags enable guests to easily learn each other's names and affiliations. It is important to recognize, however, that the use of name tags automatically suggests a certain degree of informality. For this reason, we recommend that their use be confined to business activities and less formal social events such as meetings, seminars, receptions, and other very large gatherings. Name tags are inappropriate at any seated meal (where place cards fulfill their function) or any black-tie or white-tie event.

Certain officials should not be asked to wear name tags. These include heads of state, heads of government, royalty, and very high-ranking religious officials. This is not an inflexible rule, however, and you should follow the preference of each official. It might be possible to find a president who would like to have a name tag if all the other guests do, or an official of a lower rank who would object to wearing one.

Guidelines

A name tag should meet three criteria. First, it should be easy to read, both in typeface and in content. Second, it should be as informative as possible. Third, it should display each guest's name and title in a respectful way. To best meet these standards, consider the following guidelines:

1) Prepare the tags in advance for all guests, using a large, clear typeface. Have some blank tags available at the event for unexpected guests or to replace any that may be incorrect.

2) The name tag should be worn high on the right shoulder, to be easily read while shaking hands.

3) A pin or clip-on tag generally looks neater than an adhesive one and does not leave residue on clothing.

4) The first line of the tag should contain the guest's name as it is used in conversation, as well as any professional title that he or she regularly uses. We choose to omit all honorifics (The Honorable, Her Excellency) and gender titles (Mr., Ms.) to eliminate clutter, but we include professional titles if the guest normally uses one (Dr., military titles).

5) The guest's title or affiliation belongs on the second line and should be brief enough to be quickly read but detailed enough to be correct.

For example:

> Dr. Jane Smith
> Ambassador of New Zealand

> George Wilson
> Houston City Council Member

> Mary Wilson
> Honorary Consul of Iceland

> Col. David Brown
> President, XYZ Corporation

> Bill Green
> XYZ Corporation

6) Occasionally it may be necessary to include a third line on a name tag. This is usually done when a title seems desirable but is very long.

For example:

```
┌─────────────────────────────┐
│     Phillip Jones           │
│  Vice President of Marketing │
│     XYZ Corporation         │
└─────────────────────────────┘
```

We avoid including this third line whenever possible, since the longer a name tag, the harder it is to read.

7) For spouses without official titles of their own, we recommend using full names on the first line and, for international guests, their country on the second line.

For example:

```
┌─────────────────────────────┐
│    Danielle Mitterand       │
│         France              │
└─────────────────────────────┘
```

```
┌─────────────────────────────┐
│    Dr. Maria Arteche        │
│         Spain               │
└─────────────────────────────┘
```

If the spouse's first name is unknown, "Mrs. Michael Smith" is an alternative, but avoid this by making every effort to find out the individual's first name.

Using Names and Titles in Printed Materials

A problem frequently encountered at the Protocol Alliance concerns the appropriate ways to list dignitaries in printed materials such as programs, lists of donors, letterheads, plaques, and banners. Although we cannot in this guide address all possibilities for every title, we can provide some general guidelines.

Always opt for the most formal but still practical way to address an official. Ideally, "Honorific-Full Name-Full Title" should be used at all times, yielding combinations such as "The Honorable George E. Wilson, Houston City Council Member" and "The Honorable John Brown, Former Ambassador to France." However, this may not always be possible. Perhaps the person has a long name and title but space is very limited. Perhaps the list will be read aloud and needs to be more concise. Perhaps you are making a banner or a less formal document and using "The Honorable" seems awkward.

There are many ways to deal with such situations, and you may have to try several to find the option that best suits your purposes. One way to solve the space dilemma is to abbreviate the honorific: "The Honorable" becomes "The Hon." and "His Excellency" becomes "H.E." This should be done only if the honorific must be included but does not fit any other way, since abbreviations should generally be avoided. Often it is best to just omit the honorific and use "Full Name-Full Title." This takes less space and is less repetitive if you have many elected officials to list, but it is also less formal. Another option is to use "Title-Full Name," such as "Council Member George Wilson" or "Ambassador Nancy Jones." Because the honorific must be omitted and some titles abbreviated or changed, this is appropriate only in less formal circumstances. It can also be confusing. Do you use "Houston City Council Member," "City Council Member," or "Council Member"? What happens if the same list includes "President Bill Clinton" and "President Dave Smith" (president of some group or institution)? Sometimes, particularly on certificates and plaques, just names are enough.

Whichever format you choose, it is important to be consistent. If you are using "The Honorable" for one elected official, use it for all. If you are using "Mr.," "Mrs.," and "Dr.," use them for everyone.

Using Names and Titles in Printed Materials

Double check everything. If you are including titles, make sure they are complete and correct. Be absolutely certain that all names are spelled correctly and listed as the individual prefers. Does the council member prefer "George E. Wilson" or "George Wilson"? Does Jane Smith use "Ms." or "Mrs."? Is the proper title "Ambassador of Jordan" or "Ambassador of the Hashemite Kingdom of Jordan"? You may need to ask a representative of the official.

Obviously, titles are taken seriously; otherwise the need for this book would not exist. The examples included here cover the officials whom you are most likely to encounter. Unfortunately, the most difficult situations are the ones that we cannot predict. When in doubt, ask about the office holder's preference and consider the degree of formality that you wish to convey. We have tried to err on the side of formality in these examples.

This book includes examples of former and future office holders at various levels. Often what is true for one level of government is true for all. For example, someone who has been elected to public office in the United States but has not yet been sworn in is "The Honorable George Wilson, Title-elect." Likewise, a former elected official in the United States is always entitled to be called "The Honorable." These types of generalizations may help you when there is no listing for the specific title that you seek.

For the most part, female officials are addressed just as are their male counterparts. Miss, Mrs., or Ms. is used according to the official's own preference. Though traditional etiquette rules suggest using Ms. only when a woman's marital status is unknown or when she indicates that she prefers it, it is now used commonly for all women in the United States. If you are writing to women outside of the United States, consider using Miss when in doubt, as it is both more formal and easier to translate. Incidentally, when a reference to a male official is "Mr. Title," for a woman it should be "Madam Title." Thus, "Mr. Secretary" becomes "Madam Secretary," no matter what her marital status may be.

Complications involving female office holders often arise with regard to social correspondence. Many women prefer simply to use "Mr. and Mrs. David Jones" on all social occasions, thus eliminating the confusion and adhering to tradition. However, when inviting a couple because of the woman's official title, it is important to acknowledge her position. Thus, when a woman holds an official title and her husband does not, use "The Honorable Sara Marie Jones and Mr. Jones," or whatever format is appropriate to her title. When both husband and wife hold official titles and both titles should be acknowledged, the proper form becomes "The Honorable Sara Marie Jones and The Honorable David L. Jones" if they are invited in relation to her position, or "The Honorable David L. Jones and The Honorable Sara Marie Jones" if the invitation results more from his status. You should also verify names: many women do not use their husbands' last names and some use different names in business than socially.

This checklist should help ensure error-free correspondence. It may occasionally be necessary to verify information through a third party or through the individual's office.

__ **Name:** Have you verified the individual's name and its spelling? If it is not an English name, are you sure which part is the surname? Are you using the form the person prefers: for example, Jim or James?

__ **Title:** Are you sure of the individual's full title? Have you used the guidelines in this book, or inquired elsewhere as to how to properly address this official?

__ **Country Name:** In correspondence with foreign dignitaries, check the official country name and use it where appropriate. For example, use "the Hashemite Kingdom of Jordan" rather than "Jordan" in titles and on place cards.

For social correspondence in particular:

__ **Address:** Are you mailing to the home address or the business address? Have you verified the address?

__ **Title:** The forms of address used in social correspondence may differ from those used in business correspondence. Have you ensured that you are addressing the official correctly?

__ **Spouse:** Have you clearly indicated whether or not spouses are included in the invitation? May a single official bring a guest? Have you verified the spouse's correct name and title? Many women do not take their husbands' names upon marriage, a divorcée may still be using "Mrs.," or a spouse may hold an important title of his or her own.

__ **Style:** Is the invitation envelope addressed by hand or with a reasonable facsimile of handwriting? Have you used a stamp instead of metered postage? Have you avoided all abbreviations, except for titles such as "Mr.," "Mrs.," and "Dr."?

Useful Terms

This list of terms may be helpful to you in working with the international community and with members of the consular and diplomatic corps.

Appointed Ambassador
An individual appointed by a head of state to be his or her personal representative and to represent his or her country to another.

Ambassador Designate
The title of an appointed ambassador until he or she has been approved by the receiving head of state and has taken an oath of office.

Ambassador Extraordinary and Plenipotentiary
The formal title of a representative of a head of state who has been recognized by the head of the receiving state. Before his or her accreditation, the correct description is *Ambassador Extraordinary*.

Chancery
The premises occupied by an ambassador, though *Embassy* is the term that is most commonly used.

Chargé d'Affaires
Generally, an individual who is in charge of a mission in the absence of the accredited chief of mission.

Chief of Mission
An individual who is the ranking official at a mission.

Consul (also known as a career consul)
A member of a country's foreign or consular service. This person is designated by his or her government to officially represent that government's political and commercial interests and to assist its citizens in a foreign jurisdiction. Additional duties might include developing commercial, economic, cultural, and scientific ties, as well as promoting friendly relations. Prior to his or her accreditation by the United States Department of State, the individual is considered a designated consular officer (see *Exequatur*).

Consul General
The highest position possible in a consulate, a consular officer of the highest rank (see *Rank*), and the head of post of a consulate general.

Consulate
The premises occupied by a consul. Most consulates are low-profile commercial and cultural agencies. They help channel investment dollars into a community, enhance community prestige, and bring jobs and business opportunities.

Consulate General
The term describing a consular office when the head of post holds the rank of consul general.

Counselor (also Minister-Counselor)
A ranking staff member at a mission. Minister-counselors precede counselors, who precede attachés and first and second secretaries. Some may also hold functional titles, such as Economics Minister. These titles are generally not found on the consular staff level, and care should be taken to avoid confusing a cabinet minister with the diplomatic corps rank of minister.

Deputy Chief of Mission
The second-highest ranking official at a mission; generally second only to the ambassador and often in command of the office in the absence of the chief of mission.

Diplomatic Corps
The collective group of foreign diplomatic personnel resident in a capital city.

Diplomatic Immunity
This freedom from prosecution under local law accorded to accredited diplomats is assigned by the United States Department of State according to rank and nationality and is closely regulated. It is the duty of all persons enjoying such privileges and immunities to respect local laws and regulations. Consular officers generally enjoy a limited form of immunity, called official acts immunity. For more information, see the Vienna Convention on Consular Relations, Articles 41, 43, and 71. (See also *Reciprocity*.)

Useful Terms

Embassy
The assignment of an ambassador to a foreign government. Often used to refer to the offices of an ambassador, though *Chancery* is the most appropriate term.

Exequatur
The formal act that grants the diplomatic or consular official the right to perform his or her duties in the United States.

Head of Post
The official in charge of a consulate.

Honorary Consul
A citizen of the United States or a permanent resident who represents a foreign government and performs consular services on a part-time basis, but who is not employed by the country represented and does not receive a salary.

Mission
A general term for an embassy, delegation, diplomatic office, or legation. For a sub-office or consulate, *Post* is the correct designation.

Protocol
Diplomatic etiquette or formalities (such as official ceremonies, precedence, immunities, privileges, and courtesies); the forms of ceremony and etiquette used by diplomats and government officials.

Precedence
An order of rank observed on formal occasions and extended as a courtesy on other occasions. Precedence is always used in determining seating arrangements for official functions. Failure to recognize the proper rank and precedence of an official can be construed as an insult to the official and country represented. In 1815, the Vienna Convention standardized guidelines of precedence for diplomatic officials based on rank and the date the official's credentials were recognized by the host government. Within a rank, precedence is established by the length of time at a post. Precedence and rank are personal; they cannot be transferred to

another on any occasion. For example, an official who substitutes for another at an event is given precedence according to his or her own rank, and not that of the person for whom he or she is substituting.

Rank
Official grade or position. For diplomatic corps members, the most common ranks are ambassador, minister, chargé d'affaires, counselor, attaché, and secretary. The only official categories of consular officials by rank are consul general, consul, vice consul, and consular agent, though countries are free to use their own unofficial titles— such as deputy consul, chancellor, and consular attaché— for unofficial purposes. Honorary titles follow the same general ranking as career titles. All career consular heads of post precede all honorary ones. Spouses of diplomatic officials assume the rank of that official, unless they hold a higher rank in their own right. A couple thus assumes the higher ranking of either of the two individuals.

Reciprocity
The mutual exchange between nations of privileges and rights, or occasionally their withdrawal. It is a long-standing international principle that all diplomats exchanged between two countries will enjoy roughly equivalent privileges and rights.

United States:
Federal Government

"The Honorable"

The courtesy title "The Honorable" is used in addressing most government officials. As a rule, all holders of elected office in the United States on the national, state, and local levels are given this designation, as are many presidential appointees. When addressing a letter, "The Honorable" should be written out in full on the line above the name, or immediately to the left of the name. It should not be used in a salutation or in speaking to a person, although it is sometimes used in platform introductions. According to United States usage, when using "The Honorable," the person's full name (first and last) should be used, but not Mr., Mrs., Dr., or any similar courtesy title. However, "The Honorable Dr." is occasionally used in correspondence with foreign officials.

Officials never use this courtesy title to refer to themselves, as part of their titles, or on their stationery. Generally, lower-level appointed officials are not called "The Honorable." When in doubt, however, it is appropriate to use the title as a courtesy.

Former Officials

In the United States, an elected or appointed official who leaves office loses all titles, unless he or she is a career military or foreign service officer. However, it is appropriate to continue to use "The Honorable" for former officials. Thus, a former governor is addressed as "The Honorable Mary Wilson," but no other title is used. Designations such as "Former President" and "Former Governor" are useful in making introductions or describing the individual, but are not used formally in correspondence or on place cards. Former President Bush, now resident in Houston, is still sometimes referred to as "President Bush," but this is technically incorrect and can be confusing, so avoid using it. See page 34 for an example of the preferred usage.

United States: Federal Government

The First Lady

The first lady is the one woman in the United States to whom the usual rules for addressing female officials and spouses do not apply. The president's wife is traditionally always identified by her surname; her first name is not used by others or even on her personal stationery. Thus it was always "Mrs. Bush," and never "Barbara Bush" or "Mrs. George Bush." However, the present first lady (Mrs. Clinton) has indicated that she prefers to be known as "Hillary Rodham Clinton," and her preferences should be respected. Please note also that "First Lady" is not a title in the usual sense of the word. It may be used in introductions— "May I present Mrs. Hillary Rodham Clinton, the first lady?"— but it is not used in correspondence or on place cards.

Outside the United States

When there are officials from several nations present or when American officials are out of the country, we recommend adding "of the United States" to their titles for place cards and in introductions. This helps to eliminate confusion as to which secretary of state sits at which place or which ambassador is being introduced. We prefer the addition of "of the United States" rather than the often-seen "of America" simply because the other citizens of the western hemisphere consider themselves Americans, too.

Business Correspondence

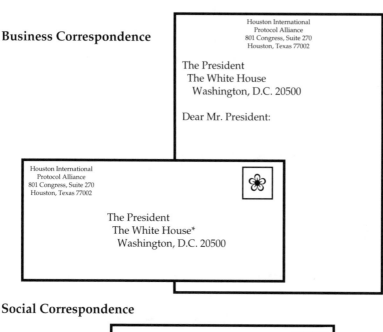

Houston International
Protocol Alliance
801 Congress, Suite 270
Houston, Texas 77002

The President
The White House
Washington, D.C. 20500

Dear Mr. President:

Houston International
Protocol Alliance
801 Congress, Suite 270
Houston, Texas 77002

The President
The White House*
Washington, D.C. 20500

Social Correspondence

*The President
and Mrs. Clinton
The White House
Washington, D.C. 20500*

Place card

The President

Introductions: The President, or The President of the United States

Conversation: Mr. President, or Sir

* It is not necessary to use "1600 Pennsylvania Avenue" in the address.

First Lady*

Business Correspondence

Houston International
Protocol Alliance
801 Congress, Suite 270
Houston, Texas 77002

Mrs. Hillary Rodham Clinton**
The White House
Washington, D.C. 20500

Dear Mrs. Clinton:

Houston International
Protocol Alliance
801 Congress, Suite 270
Houston, Texas 77002

Mrs. Hillary Rodham Clinton**
The White House
Washington, D.C. 20500

Social Correspondence

*Mrs. Hillary Rodham Clinton***
*The White House****
Washington, D.C. 20500

Place card

Mrs. Clinton

Introductions: The First Lady, Hillary Rodham Clinton**

Conversation: Mrs. Clinton, or Ma'am

* See also the information regarding the First Lady on page 30.
** In traditional usage, "Mrs. Clinton" would be used here. See page 30 for more information.
*** Use this form only when inviting the First Lady alone. If including the President, use the form shown on page 31.

Business Correspondence

Houston International
Protocol Alliance
801 Congress, Suite 270
Houston, Texas 77002

The Vice President
United States Senate
Washington, D.C. 20510

Dear Mr. Vice President:

Houston International
Protocol Alliance
801 Congress, Suite 270
Houston, Texas 77002

✿

The Vice President
United States Senate
Washington, D.C. 20510

Social Correspondence

✿

*The Vice President
and Mrs. Gore
United States Senate
Washington, D.C. 20510*

Place card

*The Vice President**

Introductions: The Vice President, or The Vice President of the
United States

Conversation: Mr. Vice President, or Sir

---

* His wife's place card would read, "Mrs. Gore."

Former President or Vice President*

Business Correspondence

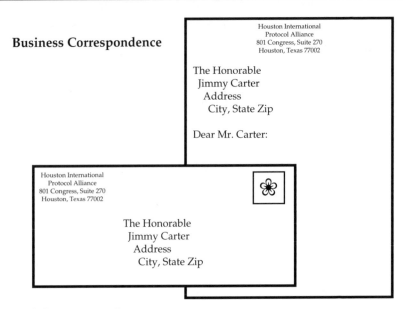

Houston International
Protocol Alliance
801 Congress, Suite 270
Houston, Texas 77002

The Honorable
Jimmy Carter
Address
City, State Zip

Dear Mr. Carter:

Houston International
Protocol Alliance
801 Congress, Suite 270
Houston, Texas 77002

The Honorable
Jimmy Carter
Address
City, State Zip

Social Correspondence

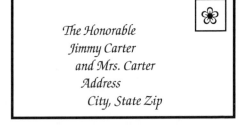

The Honorable
Jimmy Carter
and Mrs. Carter
Address
City, State Zip

Place card

Mr. Carter

Introductions: The Honorable Jimmy Carter

Conversation: Mr. Carter, or Sir

* Although "President Carter" is frequently used, it is incorrect. Presidents and vice presidents do not retain their titles upon leaving office. Usually they revert to "Mr.," but they could also use a military title or "Dr.," if they were entitled to such a designation. "The Honorable" should be used for all former presidents and vice presidents.

Business Correspondence

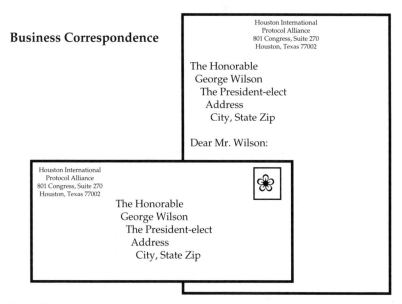

Houston International
Protocol Alliance
801 Congress, Suite 270
Houston, Texas 77002

The Honorable
George Wilson
The President-elect
Address
City, State Zip

Dear Mr. Wilson:

Houston International
Protocol Alliance
801 Congress, Suite 270
Houston, Texas 77002

The Honorable
George Wilson
The President-elect
Address
City, State Zip

Social Correspondence

The Honorable
George Wilson
and Mrs. Wilson
Address
City, State Zip

Place card

Mr. Wilson

Introductions: The Honorable George Wilson, President-elect

Conversation: Mr. Wilson

Cabinet Member

Business Correspondence

Houston International
Protocol Alliance
801 Congress, Suite 270
Houston, Texas 77002

The Honorable
George Wilson
Secretary of State
2201 C Street, N.W.
Washington, D.C. 20520

Dear Mr. Secretary:

Houston International
Protocol Alliance
801 Congress, Suite 270
Houston, Texas 77002

The Honorable
George Wilson
Secretary of State
2201 C Street, N.W.
Washington, D.C. 20520

Social Correspondence

The Honorable
The Secretary of State
and Mrs. Wilson
2201 C Street, N.W.
Washington, D.C. 20520

Place card

The Secretary of State

Introductions: The Honorable George Wilson, Secretary of State

Conversation: Mr. Secretary, or Mr. Wilson

Business Correspondence

Houston International
Protocol Alliance
801 Congress, Suite 270
Houston, Texas 77002

The Honorable
George Wilson
Under Secretary of Commerce
Department of Commerce
Address
Washington, D.C. Zip

Dear Mr. Wilson:

Houston International
Protocol Alliance
801 Congress, Suite 270
Houston, Texas 77002

The Honorable
George Wilson
Under Secretary of Commerce
Department of Commerce
Address
Washington, D.C. Zip

Social Correspondence

*The Honorable
The Under Secretary of Commerce
and Mrs. Wilson
Address
City, State Zip*

Place card

*The Under Secretary
of Commerce*

Introductions: The Honorable George Wilson, Under Secretary of Commerce

Conversation: Mr. Wilson

* In the Departments of State, Treasury, Defense, Justice, and Transportation, the position has the title of "Deputy Secretary." For those departments, use "Deputy Secretary" wherever "Under Secretary" appears above.

United States Supreme Court Chief Justice

Business Correspondence

Houston International
Protocol Alliance
801 Congress, Suite 270
Houston, Texas 77002

The Chief Justice
The Supreme Court
Washington, D.C. 20543

Dear Chief Justice:

Houston International
Protocol Alliance
801 Congress, Suite 270
Houston, Texas 77002

The Chief Justice
The Supreme Court
Washington, D.C. 20543

Social Correspondence

*The Chief Justice
and Mrs. Wilson
Address
City, State Zip*

Place card

The Chief Justice

Introductions: The Chief Justice of the Supreme Court of the United States

Conversation: Chief Justice, or Sir or Ma'am

United States Supreme Court Associate Justice

Business Correspondence

Houston International
Protocol Alliance
801 Congress, Suite 270
Houston, Texas 77002

Justice Wilson
The Supreme Court
Washington, D.C. 20543

Dear Madam Justice:*

Houston International
Protocol Alliance
801 Congress, Suite 270
Houston, Texas 77002

❁

Justice Wilson
The Supreme Court
Washington, D.C. 20543

Social Correspondence

❁

*Justice Wilson
and Mr. Wilson
Address
City, State Zip*

Place card

Justice Wilson

Introductions: Justice Wilson of the Supreme Court of the United
States

Conversation: Justice, Justice Wilson, or Sir or Ma'am

---

* The salutation for a man would be "Dear Mr. Justice." "Dear Justice Wilson" is
appropriate for both genders.

United States Senator

Business Correspondence

Houston International
Protocol Alliance
801 Congress, Suite 270
Houston, Texas 77002

The Honorable
George Wilson
United States Senate*
Washington, D.C. 20510

Dear Senator Wilson:

Houston International
Protocol Alliance
801 Congress, Suite 270
Houston, Texas 77002

The Honorable
George Wilson
United States Senate*
Washington, D.C. 20510

Social Correspondence

The Honorable
George Wilson
and Mrs. Wilson
Address
City, State Zip

Place card

Senator Wilson

Introductions: The Honorable George Wilson, United States Senator from Texas

Conversation: Senator, or Senator Wilson

* Outside of Washington, it is preferable to use "The Honorable George Wilson, United States Senator, Address."

Business Correspondence

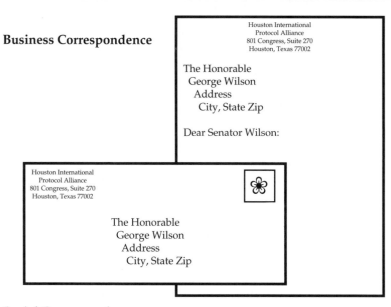

Houston International
Protocol Alliance
801 Congress, Suite 270
Houston, Texas 77002

The Honorable
George Wilson
Address
City, State Zip

Dear Senator Wilson:

Houston International
Protocol Alliance
801 Congress, Suite 270
Houston, Texas 77002

The Honorable
George Wilson
Address
City, State Zip

Social Correspondence

The Honorable
George Wilson
and Mrs. Wilson
Address
City, State Zip

Place card

Senator Wilson

Introductions: The Honorable George Wilson, former United States Senator from Texas

Conversation: Senator, or Senator Wilson

* The office of United States senator is an anomaly among former officeholders. It is still correct to use the title "Senator" in salutations and on place cards for former senators.

Business Correspondence

Houston International
Protocol Alliance
801 Congress, Suite 270
Houston, Texas 77002

The Honorable
George Wilson
United States Senate
Washington, D.C. 20510

Dear Senator Wilson:

Houston International
Protocol Alliance
801 Congress, Suite 270
Houston, Texas 77002

The Honorable
George Wilson
United States Senate
Washington, D.C. 20510

Social Correspondence

*The Honorable
George Wilson
and Mrs. Wilson
Address
City, State Zip*

Place card

Senator Wilson

Introductions: The Honorable George Wilson, United States Senator from Texas

Conversation: Senator, or Senator Wilson

Business Correspondence

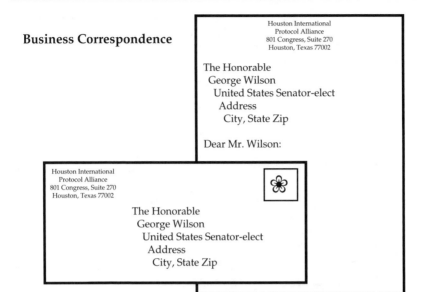

Houston International
Protocol Alliance
801 Congress, Suite 270
Houston, Texas 77002

The Honorable
George Wilson
    United States Senator-elect
    Address
        City, State Zip

Dear Mr. Wilson:

Houston International
Protocol Alliance
801 Congress, Suite 270
Houston, Texas 77002

The Honorable
George Wilson
    United States Senator-elect
    Address
        City, State Zip

Social Correspondence

*The Honorable
George Wilson
and Mrs. Wilson
Address
City, State Zip*

Place card

Mr. Wilson

Introductions: The Honorable George Wilson, United States Senator-elect from Texas

Conversation: Mr. Wilson

United States Representative

Business Correspondence

Houston International
Protocol Alliance
801 Congress, Suite 270
Houston, Texas 77002

The Honorable
Mary Wilson
    House of Representatives*
    Washington, D.C. 20515

Dear Ms. Wilson:

Houston International
Protocol Alliance
801 Congress, Suite 270
Houston, Texas 77002

❀

The Honorable
Mary Wilson
House of Representatives*
Washington, D.C. 20515

Social Correspondence

❀

The Honorable
Mary Wilson
and Mr. Wilson
Address
City, State Zip

Place card

Ms. Wilson

Introductions: The Honorable Mary Wilson, United States
Representative from Texas

Conversation: Ms. Wilson

* Outside of Washington, use the mailing address on this line; no mention of title is
needed.

Business Correspondence

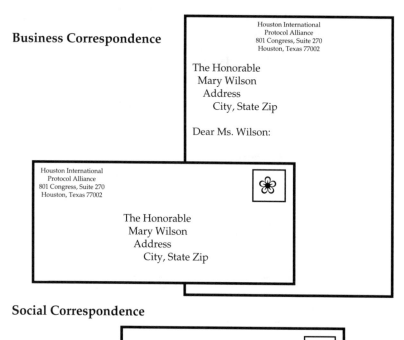

Houston International
Protocol Alliance
801 Congress, Suite 270
Houston, Texas 77002

The Honorable
Mary Wilson
Address
   City, State Zip

Dear Ms. Wilson:

Houston International
Protocol Alliance
801 Congress, Suite 270
Houston, Texas 77002

The Honorable
Mary Wilson
Address
   City, State Zip

Social Correspondence

The Honorable
Mary Wilson
and Mr. Wilson
Address
   City, State Zip

Place card

Ms. Wilson

Introductions: The Honorable Mary Wilson, former Representative from Texas

Conversation: Ms. Wilson

Business Correspondence

Houston International
Protocol Alliance
801 Congress, Suite 270
Houston, Texas 77002

The Honorable
Mary Wilson
House of Representatives
Washington, D.C. 20515

Dear Ms. Wilson:

Houston International
Protocol Alliance
801 Congress, Suite 270
Houston, Texas 77002

❁

The Honorable
Mary Wilson
House of Representatives
Washington, D.C. 20515

Social Correspondence

❁

The Honorable
Mary Wilson
and Mr. Wilson
Address
City, State Zip

Place card

Ms. Wilson

Introductions: The Honorable Mary Wilson, United States
Representative from Texas

Conversation: Ms. Wilson

Business Correspondence

Houston International
Protocol Alliance
801 Congress, Suite 270
Houston, Texas 77002

The Honorable
Mary Wilson
Speaker of the House of
Representatives
Washington, D.C. 20515

Dear Madam Speaker:

Houston International
Protocol Alliance
801 Congress, Suite 270
Houston, Texas 77002

The Honorable
Mary Wilson
Speaker of the House of
Representatives
Washington, D.C. 20515

Social Correspondence

The Speaker of the House of
Representatives
and Mr. Wilson
Address
City, State Zip

Place card

The Speaker of the
House of Representatives

Introductions: The Honorable Mary Wilson, Speaker of the
House of Representatives

Conversation: Madam Speaker, or Ma'am

United States Representative-elect

Business Correspondence

Houston International
Protocol Alliance
801 Congress, Suite 270
Houston, Texas 77002

The Honorable
Mary Wilson
Representative-elect
Address
City, State Zip

Dear Ms. Wilson:

Houston International
Protocol Alliance
801 Congress, Suite 270
Houston, Texas 77002

The Honorable
Mary Wilson
Representative-elect
Address
City, State Zip

Social Correspondence

The Honorable
Mary Wilson
and Mr. Wilson
Address
City, State Zip

Place card

Ms. Wilson

Introductions: The Honorable Mary Wilson, United States Representative-elect from Texas

Conversation: Ms. Wilson

Business Correspondence

Houston International
Protocol Alliance
801 Congress, Suite 270
Houston, Texas 77002

The Honorable
George Wilson
American Ambassador*
Address
City
Country

Dear Mr. Ambassador:

Houston International
Protocol Alliance
801 Congress, Suite 270
Houston, Texas 77002

The Honorable
George Wilson
American Ambassador*
Address
City
Country

Social Correspondence

The Honorable
*The American Ambassador**
and Guest
Address
City
Country

Place card

*The American Ambassador*****

Introductions: The Honorable George Wilson, Ambassador of the United States to Country Name

Conversation: Mr. Ambassador, or Mr. Wilson

* The term "Ambassador of the United States" is often preferred, especially in North and South America.
** The place card should read "The American Ambassador to Country Name" if he or she is not in that country or if more than one American Ambassador is present.

Former United States Ambassador

Business Correspondence

Houston International
Protocol Alliance
801 Congress, Suite 270
Houston, Texas 77002

The Honorable
Mary Wilson
Address
City, State Zip

Dear Madam Ambassador:

Houston International
Protocol Alliance
801 Congress, Suite 270
Houston, Texas 77002

The Honorable
Mary Wilson
Address
City, State Zip

Social Correspondence

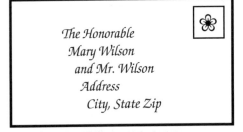

The Honorable
Mary Wilson
and Mr. Wilson
Address
City, State Zip

Place card

Ambassador Wilson

Introductions: The Honorable Mary Wilson, Former Ambassador of the United States

Conversation: Madam Ambassador, or Ms. Wilson

Business Correspondence

Houston International
Protocol Alliance
801 Congress, Suite 270
Houston, Texas 77002

Mr. George Wilson
Consul General of the United States**
Address
City
Country

Dear Mr. Wilson:

Houston International
Protocol Alliance
801 Congress, Suite 270
Houston, Texas 77002

❀

Mr. George Wilson
Consul General of the United States**
Address
City
Country

Social Correspondence

❀

Mr. and Mrs. George Wilson
Address
City
Country

Place card

Mr. Wilson

Introductions: The Consul General of the United States, Mr. Wilson**

Conversation: Mr. Wilson, or Consul General Wilson

* The same format may be used for Consuls and Vice Consuls, using those titles where appropriate.
** We prefer "Consul General of the United States," but "The American Consul General" is also used.

United States Representative to the United Nations*

Business Correspondence

Houston International
Protocol Alliance
801 Congress, Suite 270
Houston, Texas 77002

The Honorable
George Wilson
United States Representative to the
United Nations
New York, NY 10017

Dear Mr. Ambassador:

Houston International
Protocol Alliance
801 Congress, Suite 270
Houston, Texas 77002

The Honorable
George Wilson
United States Representative to the
United Nations
New York, NY 10017

Social Correspondence

*The Honorable
George Wilson
and Mrs. Wilson
Address
City, State Zip*

Place card

Mr. Wilson

Introductions: The United States Representative to the United
Nations, Ambassador Wilson

Conversation: Mr. Ambassador, or Sir

52

* The individuals who hold this position usually hold the rank of ambassador, and so
the term "Ambassador to the United Nations" is often used.

United States:
State Government

Special Considerations

Although the information in this section is applicable to all states, we have used Texas as our example. Remember that each state government has unique characteristics, so official titles may vary.

There are a few special cases you should keep in mind when working with state dignitaries outside of Texas. Although "The Honorable" (see page 29) is the preferred courtesy title in the United States, there are three states whose governors by tradition use "His/Her Excellency" (see page 85) in its place. These states are New Hampshire, South Carolina, and Massachusetts.

There are four states with official names that differ from those used in everyday conversation. Rhode Island is more formally "Rhode Island and Providence Plantation," while Pennsylvania, Kentucky, Massachusetts, and Puerto Rico (though technically the last is a territory) are "The Commonwealth of _____." These official names should be used in formal correspondence and on place cards.

Titles

There are sometimes inconsistencies in the titles of state officials. For example, "Governor of Texas" and "Governor of the State of Texas" are both used. For this book, we have chosen the form that we feel is most prevalent for each office. Variations are often permissible, and some are noted in the footnotes to the entries. In general, wherever you see "of Texas," it would be permissible to substitute "of the State of Texas."

Rank

With the exceptions of the President and Vice President of the United States, the highest ranking dignitary within any state is its governor. Outside of their home states, governors are given precedence according to each state's date of admission to the Union, or alternatively by alphabetical order according to state name.

Business Correspondence

Houston International
Protocol Alliance
801 Congress, Suite 270
Houston, Texas 77002

The Honorable
Mary Wilson
Governor of Texas
State Capitol
Austin, Texas 78711

Dear Governor Wilson:

Houston International
Protocol Alliance
801 Congress, Suite 270
Houston, Texas 77002

The Honorable
Mary Wilson
Governor of Texas
State Capitol
Austin, TX 78711

Social Correspondence

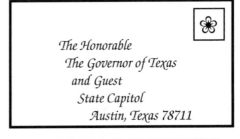

*The Honorable
The Governor of Texas
and Guest
State Capitol
Austin, Texas 78711*

Place card

The Governor of Texas

Introductions: The Honorable Mary Wilson, Governor of the State of Texas

Conversation: Governor Wilson, Governor, or Ma'am

Business Correspondence

Houston International
Protocol Alliance
801 Congress, Suite 270
Houston, Texas 77002

The Honorable
George Wilson
Address
City, State Zip

Dear Mr. Wilson:

Houston International
Protocol Alliance
801 Congress, Suite 270
Houston, Texas 77002

❀

The Honorable
George Wilson
Address
City, State Zip

Social Correspondence

❀

The Honorable
George Wilson
and Mrs. Wilson
Address
City, State Zip

Place card

Mr. Wilson

Introductions: The Honorable George Wilson, Former Governor of
Texas

Conversation: Mr. Wilson

Business Correspondence

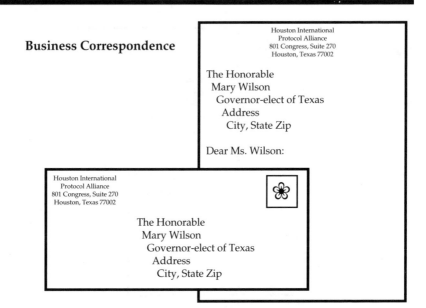

Houston International
Protocol Alliance
801 Congress, Suite 270
Houston, Texas 77002

The Honorable
Mary Wilson
Governor-elect of Texas
Address
City, State Zip

Dear Ms. Wilson:

Houston International
Protocol Alliance
801 Congress, Suite 270
Houston, Texas 77002

The Honorable
Mary Wilson
Governor-elect of Texas
Address
City, State Zip

Social Correspondence

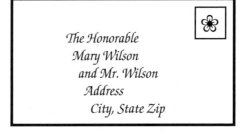

*The Honorable
Mary Wilson
and Mr. Wilson
Address
City, State Zip*

Place card

Ms. Wilson

Introductions: The Honorable Mary Wilson, Governor-elect of Texas

Conversation: Ms. Wilson

Business Correspondence

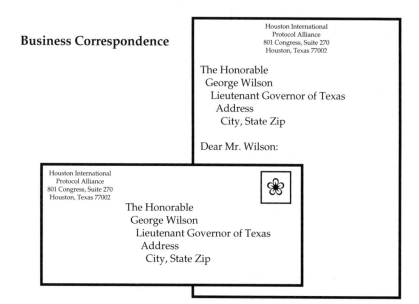

Houston International
Protocol Alliance
801 Congress, Suite 270
Houston, Texas 77002

The Honorable
George Wilson
Lieutenant Governor of Texas
Address
City, State Zip

Dear Mr. Wilson:

Houston International
Protocol Alliance
801 Congress, Suite 270
Houston, Texas 77002

The Honorable
George Wilson
Lieutenant Governor of Texas
Address
City, State Zip

Social Correspondence

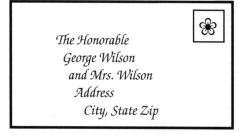

The Honorable
George Wilson
and Mrs. Wilson
Address
City, State Zip

Place card

The Lieutenant Governor
of Texas

Introductions: The Honorable George Wilson, Lieutenant Governor of Texas

Conversation: Mr. Wilson

Business Correspondence

Houston International
Protocol Alliance
801 Congress, Suite 270
Houston, Texas 77002

The Honorable
George Wilson
Secretary of State of Texas
Address
City, State Zip

Dear Mr. Secretary:

Houston International
Protocol Alliance
801 Congress, Suite 270
Houston, Texas 77002

The Honorable
George Wilson
Secretary of State of Texas
Address
City, State Zip

Social Correspondence

The Honorable
The Secretary of State of Texas
and Mrs. Wilson
Address
City, State Zip

Place card

The Secretary of State of Texas

Introductions: The Honorable George Wilson, Secretary of State of Texas

Conversation: Mr. Secretary, or Mr. Wilson

Business Correspondence

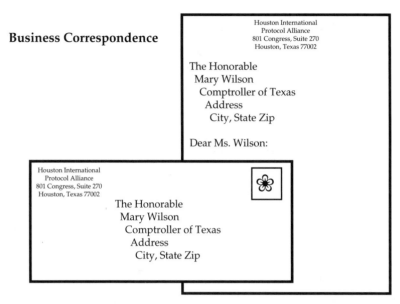

Houston International
Protocol Alliance
801 Congress, Suite 270
Houston, Texas 77002

The Honorable
Mary Wilson
 Comptroller of Texas
 Address
  City, State Zip

Dear Ms. Wilson:

Houston International
Protocol Alliance
801 Congress, Suite 270
Houston, Texas 77002

The Honorable
Mary Wilson
 Comptroller of Texas
 Address
  City, State Zip

Social Correspondence

The Honorable
Mary Wilson
and Guest
Address
City, State Zip

Place card

The Comptroller of Texas

Introductions: The Honorable Mary Wilson, Comptroller of Texas

Conversation: Ms. Wilson

Business Correspondence

Houston International
Protocol Alliance
801 Congress, Suite 270
Houston, Texas 77002

The Honorable
George Wilson
Attorney General
State of Texas
Address
   City, State Zip

Dear Mr. Attorney General:

Houston International
Protocol Alliance
801 Congress, Suite 270
Houston, Texas 77002

The Honorable
George Wilson
Attorney General
State of Texas
Address
   City, State Zip

Social Correspondence

The Honorable
The Attorney General of the
State of Texas
and Mrs. Wilson
Address
City, State Zip

Place card

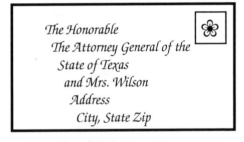

The Attorney General
of Texas

Introductions: The Honorable George Wilson, Attorney General of the State of Texas

Conversation: Mr. Attorney General, or Mr. Wilson

Business Correspondence

Houston International
Protocol Alliance
801 Congress, Suite 270
Houston, Texas 77002

The Honorable
George Wilson
Chief Justice
  Supreme Court of the State of Texas*
  Address
    City, State Zip

Dear Mr. Chief Justice:

Houston International
Protocol Alliance
801 Congress, Suite 270
Houston, Texas 77002

❀

  The Honorable
  George Wilson
  Chief Justice
    Supreme Court of the State of Texas*
    Address
      City, State Zip

Social Correspondence

❀

The Honorable
George Wilson
and Mrs. Wilson
Address
City, State Zip

Place card

The Chief Justice of Texas

Introductions: The Honorable George Wilson, Chief Justice of the Supreme Court of Texas

Conversation: Mr. Chief Justice

* "The Texas Supreme Court" is an alternative here, if space is a problem.

State Senator

Business Correspondence

Houston International
Protocol Alliance
801 Congress, Suite 270
Houston, Texas 77002

The Honorable
George Wilson
Texas Senate*
Address
City, State Zip

Dear Mr. Wilson:

Houston International
Protocol Alliance
801 Congress, Suite 270
Houston, Texas 77002

The Honorable
George Wilson
Texas Senate*
Address
City, State Zip

Social Correspondence

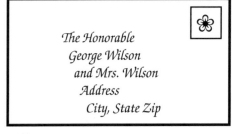

The Honorable
George Wilson
and Mrs. Wilson
Address
City, State Zip

Place card

Mr. Wilson

Introductions: The Honorable George Wilson, Texas State Senator

Conversation: Mr. Wilson

---

* "Senate of the State of Texas" is also appropriate.

Business Correspondence

Houston International
Protocol Alliance
801 Congress, Suite 270
Houston, Texas 77002

The Honorable
Mary Wilson
President of the Senate
of the State of Texas*
Address
City, State Zip

Dear Ms. Wilson:

Houston International
Protocol Alliance
801 Congress, Suite 270
Houston, Texas 77002

The Honorable
Mary Wilson
President of the Senate
of the State of Texas*
Address
City, State Zip

Social Correspondence

The Honorable
Mary Wilson
and Mr. Wilson
Address
City, State Zip

Place card

Ms. Wilson

Introductions: The Honorable Mary Wilson, President of the Senate
of the State of Texas

Conversation: Ms. Wilson

* "President of the Texas Senate" is also appropriate.

State Representative

Business Correspondence

Houston International
Protocol Alliance
801 Congress, Suite 270
Houston, Texas 77002

The Honorable
George Wilson
Texas House of Representatives*
Address
City, State Zip

Dear Mr. Wilson:

Houston International
Protocol Alliance
801 Congress, Suite 270
Houston, Texas 77002

The Honorable
George Wilson
Texas House of Representatives*
Address
City, State Zip

Social Correspondence

The Honorable
George Wilson
and Mrs. Wilson
Address
City, State Zip

Place card

Mr. Wilson

Introductions: The Honorable George Wilson, Texas State
Representative

Conversation: Mr. Wilson

* "House of Representatives of the State of Texas" is also appropriate.

Business Correspondence

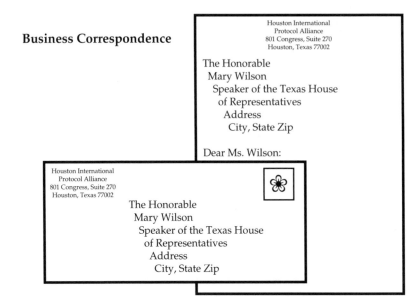

Houston International
Protocol Alliance
801 Congress, Suite 270
Houston, Texas 77002

The Honorable
Mary Wilson
   Speaker of the Texas House
   of Representatives
   Address
     City, State Zip

Dear Ms. Wilson:

Houston International
Protocol Alliance
801 Congress, Suite 270
Houston, Texas 77002

The Honorable
Mary Wilson
   Speaker of the Texas House
   of Representatives
   Address
     City, State Zip

Social Correspondence

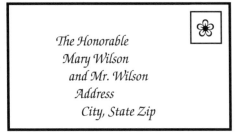

The Honorable
Mary Wilson
and Mr. Wilson
Address
City, State Zip

Place card

Ms. Wilson

Introductions: The Honorable Mary Wilson, Speaker of the Texas House of Representatives

Conversation: Ms. Wilson

United States:
Local Government

The information in this section applies to officials on the county and municipal levels. It is important to recognize that government on these levels is organized in many different ways throughout the United States. Harris County, Texas, for example, is governed by an elected county judge and a commissioners' court. Houston is led by a mayor elected at large and an elected city council and city controller. City department heads are appointed; there is no city manager.

In determining how to address officials who hold titles that are not discussed here, remember that all elected officials may be addressed as "The Honorable" (see page 29). However, appointed officials on the local level (except for judges) should not be referred to in this way.

Business Correspondence

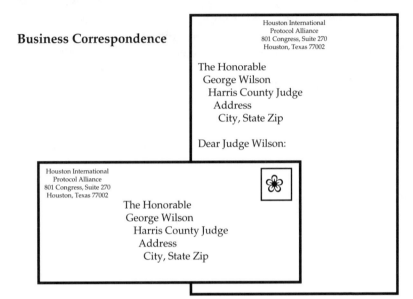

Houston International
Protocol Alliance
801 Congress, Suite 270
Houston, Texas 77002

The Honorable
George Wilson
Harris County Judge
Address
City, State Zip

Dear Judge Wilson:

Houston International
Protocol Alliance
801 Congress, Suite 270
Houston, Texas 77002

The Honorable
George Wilson
Harris County Judge
Address
City, State Zip

Social Correspondence

The Honorable
George Wilson
and Mrs. Wilson
Address
City, State Zip

Place card

Judge Wilson

Introductions: The Honorable George Wilson, Harris County Judge

Conversation: Judge Wilson

Business Correspondence

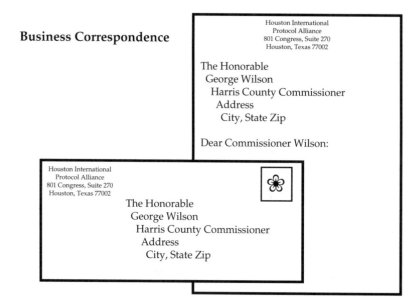

Houston International
Protocol Alliance
801 Congress, Suite 270
Houston, Texas 77002

The Honorable
George Wilson
Harris County Commissioner
Address
City, State Zip

Dear Commissioner Wilson:

Houston International
Protocol Alliance
801 Congress, Suite 270
Houston, Texas 77002

The Honorable
George Wilson
Harris County Commissioner
Address
City, State Zip

Social Correspondence

The Honorable
George Wilson
and Mrs. Wilson
Address
City, State Zip

Place card

Commissioner Wilson

Introductions: The Honorable George Wilson, Harris County
Commissioner

Conversation: Commissioner Wilson, or Mr. Wilson

County Sheriff*

Business Correspondence

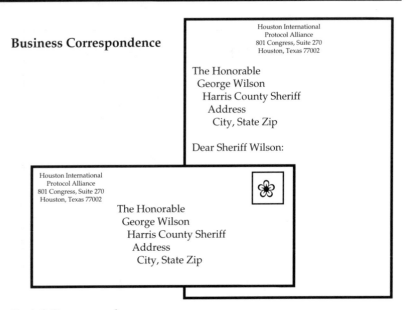

Houston International
Protocol Alliance
801 Congress, Suite 270
Houston, Texas 77002

The Honorable
George Wilson
   Harris County Sheriff
   Address
     City, State Zip

Dear Sheriff Wilson:

Houston International
Protocol Alliance
801 Congress, Suite 270
Houston, Texas 77002

The Honorable
George Wilson
   Harris County Sheriff
   Address
     City, State Zip

Social Correspondence

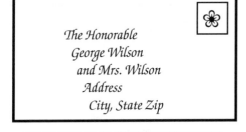

*The Honorable
George Wilson
and Mrs. Wilson
Address
City, State Zip*

Place card

Sheriff Wilson

Introductions: The Honorable George Wilson, Harris County Sheriff

Conversation: Sheriff Wilson

74

* In some areas, this is an elected position. If so, use "The Honorable." If it is not an elected office, simply use "Mr." or "Ms."

Business Correspondence

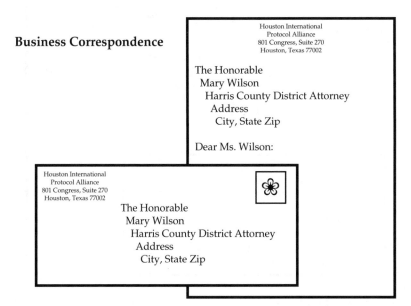

Houston International
Protocol Alliance
801 Congress, Suite 270
Houston, Texas 77002

The Honorable
Mary Wilson
Harris County District Attorney
Address
City, State Zip

Dear Ms. Wilson:

Houston International
Protocol Alliance
801 Congress, Suite 270
Houston, Texas 77002

The Honorable
Mary Wilson
Harris County District Attorney
Address
City, State Zip

Social Correspondence

The Honorable
Mary Wilson
and Mr. Wilson
Address
City, State Zip

Place card

Ms. Wilson

Introductions: The Honorable Mary Wilson, Harris County District Attorney

Conversation: Ms. Wilson

Mayor

Business Correspondence

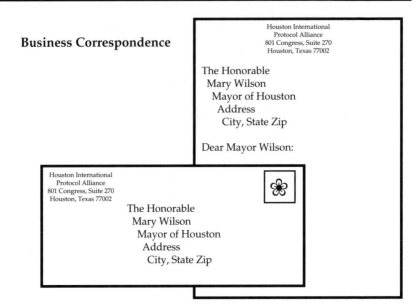

Houston International
Protocol Alliance
801 Congress, Suite 270
Houston, Texas 77002

The Honorable
Mary Wilson
  Mayor of Houston
  Address
  City, State Zip

Dear Mayor Wilson:

Houston International
Protocol Alliance
801 Congress, Suite 270
Houston, Texas 77002

The Honorable
Mary Wilson
  Mayor of Houston
  Address
  City, State Zip

Social Correspondence

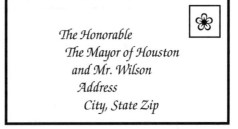

The Honorable
The Mayor of Houston
and Mr. Wilson
Address
City, State Zip

Place card

Mayor Wilson

Introductions: The Honorable Mary Wilson, Mayor of Houston

Conversation: Mayor Wilson, or Mayor

Business Correspondence

Houston International
Protocol Alliance
801 Congress, Suite 270
Houston, Texas 77002

The Honorable
George Wilson
Address
City, State Zip

Dear Mr. Wilson:

Houston International
Protocol Alliance
801 Congress, Suite 270
Houston, Texas 77002

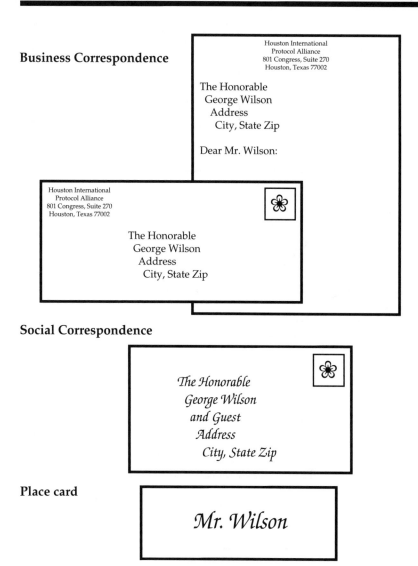

The Honorable
George Wilson
Address
City, State Zip

Social Correspondence

The Honorable
George Wilson
and Guest
Address
City, State Zip

Place card

Mr. Wilson

Introductions: The Honorable George Wilson, Former Mayor of Houston

Conversation: Mr. Wilson

Business Correspondence

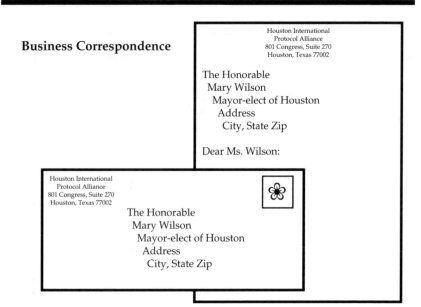

Houston International
Protocol Alliance
801 Congress, Suite 270
Houston, Texas 77002

The Honorable
Mary Wilson
    Mayor-elect of Houston
    Address
        City, State Zip

Dear Ms. Wilson:

Houston International
Protocol Alliance
801 Congress, Suite 270
Houston, Texas 77002

The Honorable
Mary Wilson
    Mayor-elect of Houston
    Address
        City, State Zip

Social Correspondence

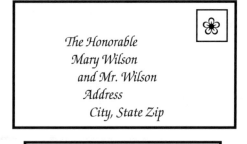

The Honorable
Mary Wilson
and Mr. Wilson
Address
City, State Zip

Place card

Ms. Wilson

Introductions: The Honorable Mary Wilson, Mayor-elect of Houston

Conversation: Ms. Wilson

Business Correspondence

Houston International
Protocol Alliance
801 Congress, Suite 270
Houston, Texas 77002

The Honorable
George Wilson
City Controller
City of Houston
Address
City, State Zip

Dear Mr. Wilson:

Houston International
Protocol Alliance
801 Congress, Suite 270
Houston, Texas 77002

The Honorable
George Wilson
City Controller
City of Houston
Address
City, State Zip

Social Correspondence

The Honorable
George Wilson
and Mrs. Wilson
Address
City, State Zip

Place card

Mr. Wilson

Introductions: The Honorable George Wilson, Houston City Controller

Conversation: Mr. Wilson

City Council Member*

Business Correspondence

Houston International
Protocol Alliance
801 Congress, Suite 270
Houston, Texas 77002

The Honorable
Mary Wilson
Council Member
City of Houston
Address
City, State Zip

Dear Ms. Wilson:

Houston International
Protocol Alliance
801 Congress, Suite 270
Houston, Texas 77002

The Honorable
Mary Wilson
Council Member
City of Houston
Address
City, State Zip

Social Correspondence

The Honorable
Mary Wilson
and Mr. Wilson
Address
City, State Zip

Place card

*Ms. Wilson***

Introductions: The Honorable Mary Wilson, Houston City Council Member

Conversation: Ms. Wilson, or Council Member Wilson

---

* We prefer to use this form when working with the Houston City Council, as we like to use gender-neutral terminology where possible. However, "Councilman" and "Councilwoman" are also used quite often, and are also correct.
** "Council Member Wilson" would also be appropriate here.

Business Correspondence

Houston International
Protocol Alliance
801 Congress, Suite 270
Houston, Texas 77002

The Honorable
George Wilson
Director and Presiding Judge
Municipal Courts
City of Houston
Address
City, State Zip

Dear Judge Wilson:

Houston International
Protocol Alliance
801 Congress, Suite 270
Houston, Texas 77002

The Honorable
George Wilson
Director and Presiding Judge
Municipal Courts
City of Houston
Address
City, State Zip

Social Correspondence

*The Honorable
George Wilson
and Mrs. Wilson
Address
City, State Zip*

Place card

Judge Wilson

Introductions: The Honorable George Wilson, Director and Presiding Judge, Municipal Courts of Houston

Conversation: Judge Wilson

Foreign Government Officials

Country Names

When dealing with foreign goverment officials, use the official name of a country whenever possible, particularly in formal correspondence. For example, use "The Republic of France" and "The Hashemite Kingdom of Jordan," not "France" and "Jordan." To verify the appropriate name, refer to the State Department's *Diplomatic List* or other publications.

There are a few nations for which the name of the country in adjective form precedes the title of ambassador. They are Sweden, Brazil, China, Malawi, the United Kingdom, and Nepal. Therefore, instead of "His Excellency, the Ambassador of the People's Republic of China," it would be proper to use "The Chinese Ambassador" (or "The British Ambassador," or "The Nepalese Ambassador," and so on.) This is not appropriate for other titles: for example, use "The President of Sweden," not "The Swedish President."

"Excellency"

"Excellency" is the courtesy title of choice around the world, preferred by all nations except the United States and members of the British Commonwealth, which use "The Honorable" (see page 29) and "The Right Honorable" (see page 86), respectively. All highly ranked dignitaries from other nations, including all heads of state, heads of government, cabinet ministers, and ambassadors, are entitled to this courtesy title. "His Excellency" or "Her Excellency" are most common, but "Excellency" is also used. This title is sometimes used in its abbreviated form of "H.E." Although this abbreviation is permissible when required by space limitations, it should be avoided where possible.

"The Honorable" may be used for any ranking foreign official who is not entitled to "Excellency." It is used, for example, to refer to most senior-level embassy officials, and in Houston we have adopted its use for the resident consular corps.

Foreign Government Officials

United Kingdom and Commonwealth Nations

In the United Kingdom and the British Commonwealth, "The Right Honorable" is generally preferred to "His Excellency." The exception is for the rank of ambassador, which does use "His Excellency." The Commonwealth of Nations includes many countries around the world, so verify each individual's preference and the customs of each nation when in doubt as to which courtesy title to use.

Sets of initials frequently follow the names of British officials. These designate the office holder's memberships in orders of knighthood and religious orders, as well as any medals, decorations, or other distinctions he or she may hold. There are many such distinctions, and they are generally used as academic degree initials (such as M.D. and Ph.D.) are in the United States. For a list of the meanings of these initials, see pages 26 and 27 of *Protocol: The Complete Handbook of Diplomatic, Official, and Social Usage*, by Mary Jane MacCaffree and Pauline Innis, or *Debrett's Correct Form*, edited by Patrick Montague-Smith.

Consular and Diplomatic Corps

The information in this section includes forms of address for foreign diplomatic and consular officials. The United States Department of State publishes the *Diplomatic List*, which includes the names and addresses of all foreign diplomats resident in Washington, D.C. A directory of United States diplomats posted overseas is also available, as is a directory of foreign consular officials in the United States. The glossary of terms on pages 22–25 of this book may also be helpful.

Titles

When corresponding with an official, it is very important to note any titles that he or she may hold. For example, "Dr." is a frequent designation in many countries around the world. The degrees that accompany this title may vary in each nation, but its usage should never be ignored. Since you may not be aware of the full significance of a given title, do not try to translate a foreign title into English if there is any doubt concerning its United States equivalent.

Place cards

Writing place cards for events that include dignitaries from other nations can be challenging. The highest-ranking dignitaries should have only titles, not names, on their place cards. If there is a United States official and one or more foreign officials with the same title (such as President, Ambassador, or Secretary), use the title and add the country name: for example, "The Ambassador of Spain." This will avoid confusion of the two officials. If there is no United States official with the same title (such as Prime Minister, Minister, or Chancellor), use the title alone: for example, "The Minister of International Trade." However, add the country name if there is more than one individual with that title present: for example, "The Minister of International Trade of Japan" and "The Minister of International Trade of Canada." For more information on place cards, see page 12.

Names

The way in which names are written differs from country to country. If you are not familiar with an individual and his or her language, correspondence may be challenging. It can be difficult to determine what part of a name is the "last" name, whether the writer is male or female, or what his or her full title is.

In many Asian countries, including China and Korea, what appears to be the person's first name may actually be his or her family name— the equivalent to an American's last name. Thus, Wang Zhijian is "Mr. Wang." However, some officials of these countries have adopted the western style while residing in or doing business in the United States. Consequently, always check and make sure that you have correctly designated the individual's last name.

Names from other cultures can also present a challenge. In most Latin American countries, full last names usually include both the mother's and the father's family names, but there are several variations. In the most common form, the father's family name is first, and this is what we would consider the "last" or family name, with the mother's family name following. Thus, Mayor Manuel Camacho Solís would be less formally referred to as Mayor Camacho, not Mayor Solís. Sometimes people use an older form, inserting "y" between the family names: Juan Ortega y Valdez, or Mr. Ortega.

It is also possible to use both names. Thus, Miguel Ruiz Morales would be referred to as "Mr. Ruiz Morales." Another option is to hyphenate. Ricardo Fernandez-Bravo is "Mr. Fernandez-Bravo." Many people choose to use just their paternal last names to avoid this confusion: for example, Luis Perez y Gomez may elect to go by "Luis Perez." Unfortunately, it is not always clear whether a name represents one family name or two: for example, should Juan Carlos Sanchez de la Torre be referred to as "Mr. Sanchez" or "Mr. Sanchez de la Torre"?

In Latin American culture, married women typically retain their paternal last names and add their husbands' paternal last names. Thus, when Alicia Morales Ortega marries Ricardo Ramirez y Vallejo, she becomes Alicia Morales de Ramirez, or Mrs. Ramirez.

In Arab culture, names follow a particular pattern. A full name may include all of these elements: Given Name/Father's Given Name/Paternal Grandfather's Given Name/Mother's Surname/Father's Surname. "Ibn" or "Bin" means "son of"; "Bint" means "daughter of." The prefixes "El-" and "Al-" denote belonging to the family names they accompany. Thus, Mohammed Bin Abdul Bin Talal Al-Said Al-Nazir's name tells us a great deal about his heritage. Arab women generally retain their own names when they marry, but it is acceptable to use "Mrs. Husband's Last Name" in social circumstances.

In many countries, women do not use their husbands' names as frequently as do women in the United States. In some cultures, women retain their own names when they marry; in others they add their husbands' surnames but would never use their first names, as in "Mrs. George Wilson." Socially, however, it is generally appropriate to call a married woman "Mrs. Husband's Last Name." This is particularly true on invitations that are being sent to the couple, or when you do not know the wife's name.

European, Asian, and African names can be just as confusing as those mentioned above. There is often no way to tell which is a person's "last" name without asking. Follow each individual's preference as best you can.

President of a Foreign Country

Business Correspondence

Houston International
Protocol Alliance
801 Congress, Suite 270
Houston, Texas 77002

His Excellency
George Wilson
President of Country Name
Address
City
Country

Dear Mr. President:

Houston International
Protocol Alliance
801 Congress, Suite 270
Houston, Texas 77002

His Excellency
George Wilson
President of Country Name
Address
City
Country

Social Correspondence

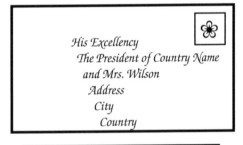

His Excellency
The President of Country Name
and Mrs. Wilson
Address
City
Country

Place card

The President
of Country Name

Introductions: His Excellency George Wilson, President of Country Name

Conversation: Your Excellency, or Mr. President

Business Correspondence

Houston International
Protocol Alliance
801 Congress, Suite 270
Houston, Texas 77002

His Excellency
George Wilson
Prime Minister of Country Name
Address
City
Country

Dear Mr. Prime Minister:

Houston International
Protocol Alliance
801 Congress, Suite 270
Houston, Texas 77002

His Excellency
George Wilson
Prime Minister of Country Name
Address
City
Country

Social Correspondence

His Excellency
The Prime Minister of Country Name
and Mrs. Wilson
Address
City
Country

Place card

*The Prime Minister**

Introductions: His Excellency George Wilson, the Prime Minister of Country Name

Conversation: Your Excellency, or Mr. Prime Minister

---

* This information applies to countries that are not members of the British Commonwealth. For Commonwealth countries, see page 92.
** If more than one prime minister is present, add "of Country Name."

Prime Minister (United Kingdom & Commonwealth)

Business Correspondence

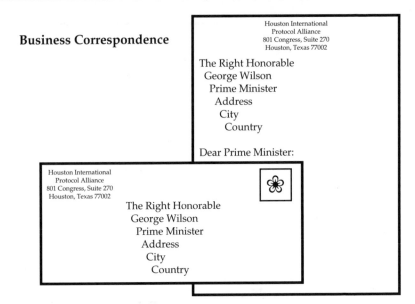

Houston International
Protocol Alliance
801 Congress, Suite 270
Houston, Texas 77002

The Right Honorable
George Wilson
Prime Minister
Address
City
Country

Dear Prime Minister:

Houston International
Protocol Alliance
801 Congress, Suite 270
Houston, Texas 77002

The Right Honorable
George Wilson
Prime Minister
Address
City
Country

Social Correspondence

The Right Honorable
The Prime Minister
and Mrs. Wilson
Address
City
Country

Place card

*The Prime Minister**

Introductions: The Right Honorable George Wilson, Prime Minister and First Lord of the Treasury of the United Kingdom of Great Britain and Northern Ireland

Conversation: Mr. Prime Minister

* If more than one prime minister is present, add "of the United Kingdom."

Business Correspondence

Houston International
Protocol Alliance
801 Congress, Suite 270
Houston, Texas 77002

His Excellency
George Wilson
Deputy Prime Minister of Country Name
Address
City
Country

Dear Mr. Deputy Prime Minister:*

Houston International
Protocol Alliance
801 Congress, Suite 270
Houston, Texas 77002

❀

His Excellency
George Wilson
Deputy Prime Minister of Country Name
Address
City
Country

Social Correspondence

His Excellency
The Deputy Prime Minister
of Country Name
and Mrs. Wilson
Address
City
Country

❀

Place card

The Deputy Prime Minister

Introductions: His Excellency George Wilson, the Deputy Prime
Minister of Country Name

Conversation: Your Excellency, or Mr. Deputy Prime Minister

---

* "Your Excellency" is a useful alternative here if "Mr. Deputy Prime Minister" seems awkward.

Cabinet Minister*

Business Correspondence

Houston International
Protocol Alliance
801 Congress, Suite 270
Houston, Texas 77002

His Excellency
George Wilson
Minister of Foreign Affairs
of Country Name
Address
City
Country

Dear Mr. Minister:**

Houston International
Protocol Alliance
801 Congress, Suite 270
Houston, Texas 77002

His Excellency
George Wilson
Minister of Foreign Affairs
of Country Name
Address
City
Country

Social Correspondence

His Excellency
The Minister of Foreign Affairs
of Country Name
and Mrs. Wilson
Address
City, Country

Place card

The Minister of Foreign Affairs

Introductions: His Excellency George Wilson, Minister of Foreign Affairs of Country Name

Conversation: Your Excellency, or Mr. Minister

---

* This information applies to all nations except members of the Commonwealth. For Commonwealth countries, see page 95.

** "Your Excellency" is also an appropriate salutation.

Business Correspondence

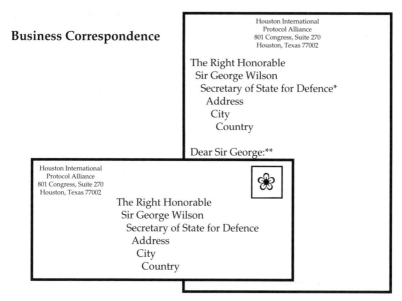

Houston International
Protocol Alliance
801 Congress, Suite 270
Houston, Texas 77002

The Right Honorable
Sir George Wilson
    Secretary of State for Defence*
    Address
    City
        Country

Dear Sir George:**

Houston International
Protocol Alliance
801 Congress, Suite 270
Houston, Texas 77002

The Right Honorable
Sir George Wilson
    Secretary of State for Defence
    Address
    City
        Country

Social Correspondence

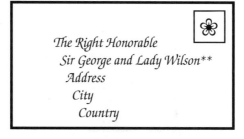

*The Right Honorable
Sir George and Lady Wilson***
*Address
City
Country*

Place card

*The Secretary of State for
Defence**

Introductions: The Right Honorable Sir George Wilson, Secretary of State for Defence*

Conversation: Mr. Secretary, or Sir George**

* We have used the British spelling of "defense" here, in order to follow the exact title of the individual as closely as possible.

** If this individual is a peer or holds a personal distinction such as knighthood, it should be noted, as in this example (see the Royalty section for more information). If the office holder is untitled, drop the "Sir" and use "Dear Mr. Wilson" and "The Right Honorable George Wilson and Mrs. Wilson."

Royalty with Official Foreign Government Position*

Business Correspondence

His Royal Highness
Prince Saud al-Faysal bin Abd al-Aziz
Minister of Foreign Affairs
of the Kingdom of Saudi Arabia
Address
City
Country

Your Royal Highness:

Houston International
Protocol Alliance
801 Congress, Suite 270
Houston, Texas 77002

His Royal Highness
Prince Saud al-Faysal bin Abd al-Aziz
Minister of Foreign Affairs
of the Kingdom of Saudi Arabia
Address
City
Country

Social Correspondence

His Royal Highness
Prince Saud al-Faysal bin Abd al-Aziz
of the Kingdom of Saudi Arabia
Address
City
Country

Place card

His Royal Highness
Prince Saud al-Faysal

Introductions: His Royal Highness Prince Saud al-Faysal bin Abd al-Aziz, Minister of Foreign Affairs of the Kingdom of Saudi Arabia

Conversation: Your Royal Highness, or Sir

---

* Royal status generally takes precedence over other titles. Include the ministerial title where possible, but use the royal forms of address.

Business Correspondence

Houston International
Protocol Alliance
801 Congress, Suite 270
Houston, Texas 77002

The Honorable*
George Wilson
Under Secretary of Energy
of Country Name
Address
City
Country

Dear Mr. Wilson:**

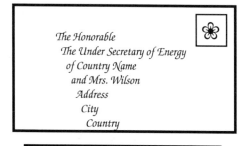

Houston International
Protocol Alliance
801 Congress, Suite 270
Houston, Texas 77002

The Honorable*
George Wilson
Under Secretary of Energy
of Country Name
Address
City
Country

Social Correspondence

The Honorable
The Under Secretary of Energy
of Country Name
and Mrs. Wilson
Address
City
Country

Place card

The Under Secretary of
Energy

Introductions: The Honorable George Wilson, Under Secretary of
Energy of Country Name

Conversation: Mr. Wilson

* Although we have used "The Honorable" here, some officials with this rank use "His
Excellency," so check the proper form for each individual.
** It might also be appropriate to use "Dear Mr. Under Secretary" here, or "Your
Excellency," if it applies.

Member of Parliament*

Business Correspondence

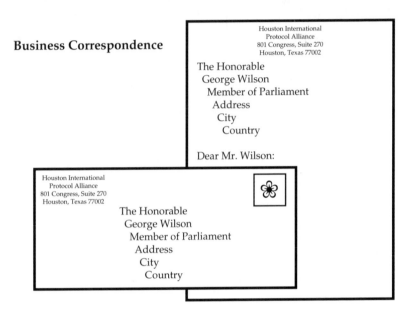

Houston International
Protocol Alliance
801 Congress, Suite 270
Houston, Texas 77002

The Honorable
George Wilson
Member of Parliament
Address
City
Country

Dear Mr. Wilson:

Houston International
Protocol Alliance
801 Congress, Suite 270
Houston, Texas 77002

The Honorable
George Wilson
Member of Parliament
Address
City
Country

Social Correspondence

The Honorable
George Wilson
and Mrs. Wilson
Address
City
Country

Place card

Mr. Wilson

Introductions: The Honorable George Wilson, Member of Parliament of Country Name

Conversation: Mr. Wilson

* For Commonwealth nations, see page 99.

Business Correspondence

Houston International
Protocol Alliance
801 Congress, Suite 270
Houston, Texas 77002

George Wilson, M.P.**
House of Commons
Address
City
Country

Dear Mr. Wilson:

Houston International
Protocol Alliance
801 Congress, Suite 270
Houston, Texas 77002

George Wilson, M.P.**
House of Commons
Address
City
Country

Social Correspondence

Mr. and Mrs. George Wilson
Address
City
Country

Place card

Mr. Wilson

Introductions: Mr. George Wilson, Member of Parliament

Conversation: Mr. Wilson

---

* As for a British cabinet member, use any personal titles the office holder may have.
** "M.P." is the abbreviation for "Member of Parliament," and it is used much more frequently in correspondence than is the entire phrase.

Business Correspondence

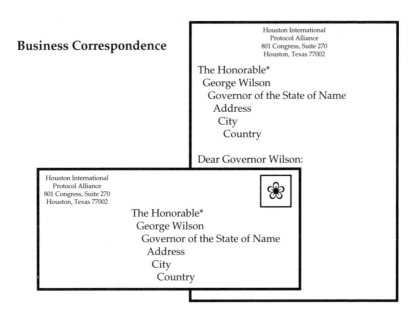

Houston International
Protocol Alliance
801 Congress, Suite 270
Houston, Texas 77002

The Honorable*
George Wilson
   Governor of the State of Name
   Address
    City
     Country

Dear Governor Wilson:

Houston International
Protocol Alliance
801 Congress, Suite 270
Houston, Texas 77002

The Honorable*
George Wilson
   Governor of the State of Name
   Address
    City
     Country

Social Correspondence

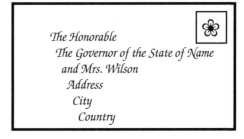

The Honorable
The Governor of the State of Name
and Mrs. Wilson
Address
City
Country

Place card

Governor Wilson

Introductions: The Honorable George Wilson, Governor of the State of Name

Conversation: Governor Wilson

---

* In some countries, governors use "Your Excellency" instead of "The Honorable." In such cases, it is appropriate to use "Your Excellency" in the salutation and in speaking.

Business Correspondence

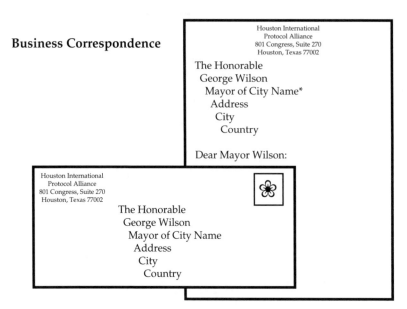

Houston International
Protocol Alliance
801 Congress, Suite 270
Houston, Texas 77002

The Honorable
George Wilson
Mayor of City Name*
Address
City
Country

Dear Mayor Wilson:

Houston International
Protocol Alliance
801 Congress, Suite 270
Houston, Texas 77002

The Honorable
George Wilson
Mayor of City Name
Address
City
Country

Social Correspondence

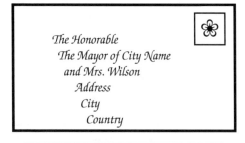

*The Honorable
The Mayor of City Name
and Mrs. Wilson
Address
City
Country*

Place card

Mayor Wilson

Introductions: The Honorable George Wilson, Mayor of City Name

Conversation: Mayor Wilson

* In some cities, "Lord Mayor" or another variation is used.

Foreign Ambassador*

Business Correspondence

Houston International
Protocol Alliance
801 Congress, Suite 270
Houston, Texas 77002

His Excellency
George Wilson
Ambassador of Country Name
Address
City
Country

Dear Mr. Ambassador:**

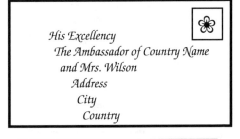

Houston International
Protocol Alliance
801 Congress, Suite 270
Houston, Texas 77002

His Excellency
George Wilson
Ambassador of Country Name
Address
City
Country

Social Correspondence

His Excellency
The Ambassador of Country Name
and Mrs. Wilson
Address
City
Country

Place card

The Ambassador of Country Name

Introductions: His Excellency George Wilson, the Ambassador of Country Name

Conversation: Mr. Ambassador, or Your Excellency

---

* For a female ambassador, use "Her Excellency" and "Madam Ambassador."
** "Your Excellency" is also appropriate as a salutation.

Business Correspondence

Houston International
Protocol Alliance
801 Congress, Suite 270
Houston, Texas 77002

The Honorable
George Wilson
    Chargé d'Affaires (ad interim) of (Country)
    Address
    City, State Zip

Dear Mr. Chargé d'Affaires:

Houston International
Protocol Alliance
801 Congress, Suite 270
Houston, Texas 77002

The Honorable
George Wilson
    Chargé d'Affaires (ad interim) of (Country)
    Address
    City, State Zip

Social Correspondence

The Honorable
The Chargé d'Affaires (ad interim)
of (Country)
and Mrs. Wilson
Address
City, State Zip

Place card

The Chargé d'Affaires (ad interim)
of Country Name

Introductions: The Honorable George Wilson, Chargé d'Affaires
of Country Name

Conversation: Mr. Chargé d'Affaires, or Mr. Wilson

---

* This format applies also to chargés d'affaires ad interim or pro tempore, inserting those
terms where appropriate, as shown.

Foreign Embassy Minister/Minister-Counselor*

Business Correspondence

Houston International
Protocol Alliance
801 Congress, Suite 270
Houston, Texas 77002

The Honorable
George Wilson
Minister
Embassy of Country Name**
Address
City, State Zip

Dear Mr. Wilson:

Houston International
Protocol Alliance
801 Congress, Suite 270
Houston, Texas 77002

The Honorable
George Wilson
Minister
Embassy of Country Name
Address
City, State Zip

Social Correspondence

The Honorable
George Wilson
and Mrs. Wilson
Address
City, State Zip

Place card

Mr. Wilson

Introductions: The Honorable George Wilson, Minister of the
Embassy of Country Name

Conversation: Mr. Wilson

* This format is appropriate for most other embassy staff members with official ranks, including counselors and attachés.
** We prefer to use "Embassy of," rather than "Minister of," which might be confused with the cabinet rank of minister.

Business Correspondence

Houston International
Protocol Alliance
801 Congress, Suite 270
Houston, Texas 77002

The Honorable**
George Wilson
Consul General of Country Name
Address
City, State Zip

Dear Consul General Wilson:

Houston International
Protocol Alliance
801 Congress, Suite 270
Houston, Texas 77002

The Honorable**
George Wilson
Consul General of Country Name
Address
City, State Zip

Social Correspondence

The Honorable
George Wilson
and Mrs. Wilson
Address
City, State Zip

Place card

*Consul General Wilson****

Introductions: The Honorable George Wilson, Consul General of Country Name

Conversation: Consul General Wilson, or Mr. Wilson

* "Consul General" is the usual title for this position, though it may be held by a consul, vice consul, or consular agent.
** In Houston, we have extended the courtesy title of "The Honorable" to heads of post as a courtesy. This was a local decision not based on U.S. State Department policy.
*** It is often helpful to add "of Country Name" to the place card as an aid to conversation.

Honorary Consul (Head of Post)*

Business Correspondence

Houston International
Protocol Alliance
801 Congress, Suite 270
Houston, Texas 77002

The Honorable
Mary Wilson
   Honorary Consul of Country Name
   Address
    City, State Zip

Dear Ms. Wilson:

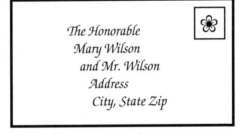

Houston International
Protocol Alliance
801 Congress, Suite 270
Houston, Texas 77002

The Honorable
Mary Wilson
   Honorary Consul of Country Name
   Address
    City, State Zip

Social Correspondence

The Honorable
Mary Wilson
and Mr. Wilson
Address
City, State Zip

Place card

*Ms. Wilson***

Introductions: The Honorable Mary Wilson, Honorary Consul of Country Name

Conversation: Ms. Wilson

---

* The only change for an honorary consular official who is not a head of post is the omission of "The Honorable."

** It would also be appropriate to use "Honorary Consul Wilson of Country Name."

Consular Official other than Head of Post*

Business Correspondence

Houston International
Protocol Alliance
801 Congress, Suite 270
Houston, Texas 77002

Mr. George Wilson
Consul of Country Name
Address
City, State Zip

Dear Mr. Wilson:**

Houston International
Protocol Alliance
801 Congress, Suite 270
Houston, Texas 77002

✿

Mr. George Wilson
Consul of Country Name
Address
City, State Zip

Social Correspondence

✿

Mr. and Mrs. George Wilson
Address
City, State Zip

Place card

*Consul Wilson****

Introductions: Mr. George Wilson, Consul of Country Name

Conversation: Mr. Wilson, or Consul Wilson

* This includes Deputy Consul, Vice Consul, and all other ranks.
** "Dear Consul Wilson" is also appropriate.
*** You might wish to add "of Country Name" to the place card as an aid to conversation.

Secretary General of the United Nations

Business Correspondence

His Excellency
George Wilson
Secretary General of the United Nations
Address
City
Country

Dear Mr. Secretary General:

His Excellency
George Wilson
Secretary General of the United Nations
Address
City
Country

Social Correspondence

His Excellency
The Secretary General
of the United Nations
and Mrs. Wilson
Address
City
Country

Place card

The Secretary General of the
United Nations

Introductions: His Excellency George Wilson, Secretary General of the United Nations

Conversation: Your Excellency, or Mr. Secretary General

Business Correspondence

Houston International
Protocol Alliance
801 Congress, Suite 270
Houston, Texas 77002

Her Excellency
Mary Wilson
Representative of Country Name
to the United Nations
Address
City
Country

Dear Madam Ambassador:

Houston International
Protocol Alliance
801 Congress, Suite 270
Houston, Texas 77002

❀

Her Excellency
Mary Wilson
Representative of Country Name
to the United Nations
Address
City
Country

Social Correspondence

Her Excellency
Mary Wilson
and Mr. Wilson
Address
City
Country

❀

Place card

The Representative of Country Name
*to the United Nations***

Introductions: Her Excellency Mary Wilson, the Representative of
Country Name to the United Nations

Conversation: Your Excellency, or Madam Ambassador

* The holders of this position normally have the rank of ambassador, as illustrated here.
** "H.E. Mary Wilson" would be a space-saving alternative.

Royalty

This section discusses the proper ways to address members of royalty from all nations. Because the British and Western European monarchies are the systems that we in the United States seem to have the most contact with, they are used in many of our examples. However, the traditions of Asian, African, or Middle Eastern royalty are often quite different. With a little caution, the information shown here can be readily applied to most royals.

Verifying Titles

Whenever working with royalty, verify the individual's title preference and educate yourself about his or her place in the royalty of that country. Find out if the country has a ruling monarch, or if the monarchy no longer plays even a ceremonial role. The embassy, consulate, or State Department can be of great assistance in this area. If the individual is not part of a ruling family, you might like to determine if the title is inherited, purchased, or honorarily awarded. This will help you avoid any confusion or embarrassment, and ensure that you properly recognize the individual.

Correspondence with Royalty

Correspondents are generally discouraged from writing directly to any member of a royal family with whom they are not personally acquainted. In most cases, it is preferable to direct all written correspondence with royals to their private secretaries, equerries, chamberlains, or ladies-in-waiting. The proper way to do this is described on page 116.

In practice, however, it may sometimes be necessary to write to the royal directly, so the proper ways to do this are also described in this section.

When writing about or speaking about royals, certain grammatical conventions should be followed. All written and spoken references to royalty should be made in the third person. For example, Queen Elizabeth should be referred to as "Her Majesty" the first time, and subsequently as "the Queen." Instead of "she" and "her," use "Her Majesty" and "Her Majesty's." The same is true for other royals, using their appropriate titles: for example, "Her Royal Highness," "His Highness," and "His Imperial Majesty's."

Titles and Honorifics

The examples illustrated here are useful for addressing royalty of many nations. For example, "Crown Prince" refers to the person who is first in line for the throne and who, in most cases, has been formally named as the successor to the current ruler. However, many more variations on these titles, and particularly on the honorifics that accompany them, are possible than we are able to include here. For example, in one nation the crown prince may be addressed as "His Royal Highness." In another, he might be "His Imperial Highness." Verify the preferences of each nation if you have any questions regarding a specific individual.

Many royals have not just one title but several. For example, Queen Elizabeth has a different title in each Commonwealth nation. In the United Kingdom, she is "Elizabeth the Second, by the Grace of God of the United Kingdom of Great Britain and Northern Ireland and of Her Other Realms and Territories Queen, Head of the Commonwealth, Defender of the Faith." The title that you use depends on the country you are in and the formality of the circumstances. In most cases, just "Her Majesty Queen Elizabeth II" is sufficient. Likewise, Prince Philip is "His Royal Highness, the Prince Philip, Duke of Edinburgh," but in his case the entire title is usually used. You should follow the individual's preference and the prevailing usage in determining which title or additional titles, if any, to use.

The Peerage

Though peers are not considered to be royals, we have included information applicable to them in this section of the book. If you have many contacts in the United Kingdom, you may at some point confront the titles of the peerage, a system of titles of which some are inherited and some are not. Because we lack an analogous system, the ranks and titles of peers seem to cause great headaches in the United States. For a detailed explanation of the various peerages, grades, and styles of address for family members, *Debrett's Correct Form* is very helpful.

On most occasions, though, you will not need to know the full history and hierarchy of the peerage. It should suffice to be aware of two basic facts. First, know the appropriate full title of the individual. This is particularly important for peers, because some hold more than one peerage, and family names and geographic distinctions play varying roles in titles. Second, keep in mind the five grades of peers, and the equivalent titles for female holders of these titles. They are, in descending order:

Duke	Duchess
Marquess	Marchioness
Earl	Countess
Viscount	Viscountess
Baron	Baroness

Although they are not considered to be part of the peerage, we have also included information on addressing baronets and knights.

British peerage titles are used in these examples, but similar titles are found in Scotland and in other countries. The devolution of such titles varies widely from country to country and they are sometimes not even recognized by that country's present government. Many times, the forms of address will be the same as those included here, but use caution, since usage and personal preferences may differ in each case.

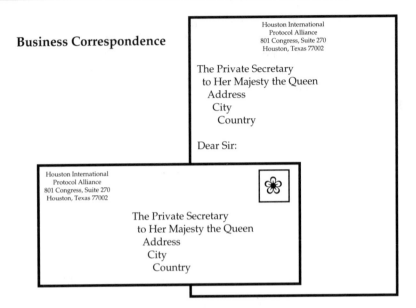

Business Correspondence

Houston International
Protocol Alliance
801 Congress, Suite 270
Houston, Texas 77002

The Private Secretary
to Her Majesty the Queen
Address
City
Country

Dear Sir:

Houston International
Protocol Alliance
801 Congress, Suite 270
Houston, Texas 77002

The Private Secretary
to Her Majesty the Queen
Address
City
Country

When addressing your initial letter, write to the holder of the office using his or her title and not name, unless you are already acquainted with that person. In all subsequent letters, you may write to the author of the reply to your first letter, using his or her name and title as you would for any other business letter.

All written and spoken references to royalty should be made in the third person. For example, Queen Elizabeth should be referred to as "Her Majesty" the first time, and subsequently as "the Queen." Instead of "she" and "her," use "Her Majesty" and "Her Majesty's." The same is true for other royals: for example, "Her Royal Highness," "His Highness," and "His Imperial Majesty's."

Business Correspondence

Houston International
Protocol Alliance
801 Congress, Suite 270
Houston, Texas 77002

Her Majesty
    Queen Elizabeth II
    Address
    City
    Country

Your Majesty:**

Houston International
Protocol Alliance
801 Congress, Suite 270
Houston, Texas 77002

Her Majesty
    Queen Elizabeth II
    Address
    City
    Country

❀

Social Correspondence

Her Majesty
Queen Elizabeth II
and His Royal Highness
The Prince Philip
The Duke of Edinburgh
City
Country

❀

Place card

Her Majesty
Queen Elizabeth II

Introductions: Her Majesty, Queen Elizabeth II

Conversation: Your Majesty at first, and Ma'am in prolonged
conversation

---

* The same would apply to a king, substituting "His Majesty."
** It is usually more appropriate to write to Her Majesty's private secretary. See page 113.

Royal Prince or Princess (Great Britain)*

Business Correspondence

Houston International
Protocol Alliance
801 Congress, Suite 270
Houston, Texas 77002

His Royal Highness
Prince Charles
Prince of Wales
Address
City
Country

Your Royal Highness:

Houston International
Protocol Alliance
801 Congress, Suite 270
Houston, Texas 77002

His Royal Highness
Prince Charles
Prince of Wales
Address
City
Country

Social Correspondence

Their Royal Highnesses
*The Prince and Princess of Wales*** *
Address
City
Country

Place card

His Royal Highness
The Prince of Wales

Her Royal Highness
The Princess of Wales

Introductions: His Royal Highness, the Prince of Wales
Her Royal Highness, the Princess of Wales

Conversation: Your Royal Highness, or Sir or Ma'am

---

* Forms of address may vary slightly outside of Britain. See, for example, page 130.
** This may vary if one spouse holds a title other than Prince or Princess. For an example, see page 117.

Business Correspondence

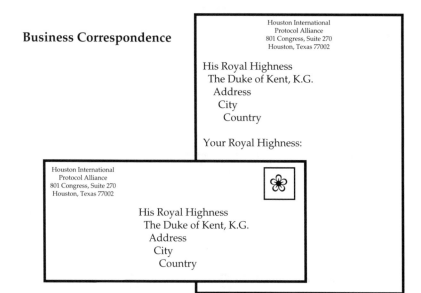

Houston International
Protocol Alliance
801 Congress, Suite 270
Houston, Texas 77002

His Royal Highness
The Duke of Kent, K.G.
Address
City
Country

Your Royal Highness:

Houston International
Protocol Alliance
801 Congress, Suite 270
Houston, Texas 77002

His Royal Highness
The Duke of Kent, K.G.
Address
City
Country

Social Correspondence

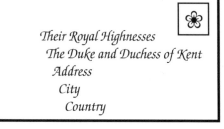

Their Royal Highnesses
The Duke and Duchess of Kent
Address
City
Country

Place card

His Royal Highness *The Duke of Kent*	*Her Royal Highness* *The Duchess of Kent*

Introductions: His Royal Highness, the Duke of Kent
Her Royal Highness, the Duchess of Kent

Conversation: Your Royal Highness, or Sir or Ma'am

The Queen Mother (Great Britain)

Business Correspondence

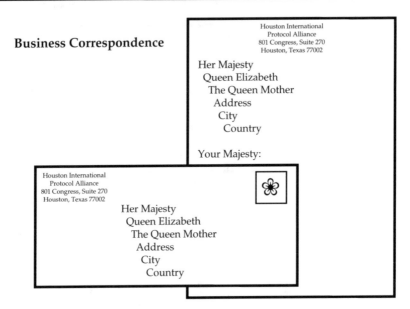

Houston International
Protocol Alliance
801 Congress, Suite 270
Houston, Texas 77002

Her Majesty
Queen Elizabeth
The Queen Mother
Address
City
Country

Your Majesty:

Houston International
Protocol Alliance
801 Congress, Suite 270
Houston, Texas 77002

Her Majesty
Queen Elizabeth
The Queen Mother
Address
City
Country

Social Correspondence

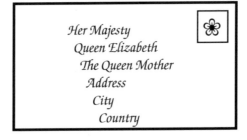

Her Majesty
Queen Elizabeth
The Queen Mother
Address
City
Country

Place card

Her Majesty Queen Elizabeth
The Queen Mother

Introductions: Her Majesty, Queen Elizabeth, the Queen Mother

Conversation: Your Majesty, or Ma'am

Business Correspondence

Houston International
Protocol Alliance
801 Congress, Suite 270
Houston, Texas 77002

His Grace*
The Duke of Somerset
Address
Country

Dear Duke:

Houston International
Protocol Alliance
801 Congress, Suite 270
Houston, Texas 77002

❀

His Grace*
The Duke of Somerset
Address
Country

Social Correspondence

❀

The Duke and Duchess of Somerset
Address
Country

Place card

The Duke of Somerset

Introductions: His Grace,* the Duke of Somerset

Conversation: Your Grace,* or Duke

* "His/Your Grace" is the traditional honorific for dukes; it is not used for other peerage titles. Although its use is still favored by many in the United Kingdom, it is now less often used, especially in the United States. If the individual is entitled to another honorific (for example, "His Excellency" or "General") it takes the place of "His Grace."

Duchess

Business Correspondence

Houston International
Protocol Alliance
801 Congress, Suite 270
Houston, Texas 77002

Her Grace*
  The Duchess of Somerset
  Address
  Country

Dear Duchess:

Houston International
Protocol Alliance
801 Congress, Suite 270
Houston, Texas 77002

Her Grace*
  The Duchess of Somerset
  Address
  Country

Social Correspondence

*Her Grace**
The Duchess of Somerset
Address
Country

Place card

The Duchess of Somerset

Introductions: Her Grace,* the Duchess of Somerset

Conversation: Your Grace,* or Duchess**

* "Her/Your Grace" is the traditional honorific for duchesses; it is not used for other peerage titles. Although its use is still favored by many in the United Kingdom, it is now less often used, especially in the United States.
** A duchess is always referred to as "The Duchess of (Somerset)" or "the Duchess," but not "Lady (Somerset)."

Business Correspondence

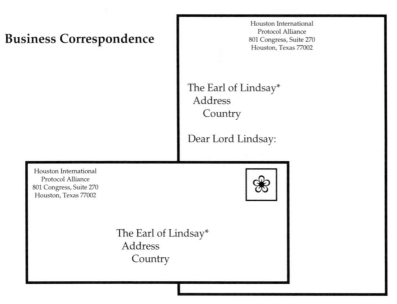

Houston International
Protocol Alliance
801 Congress, Suite 270
Houston, Texas 77002

The Earl of Lindsay*
Address
Country

Dear Lord Lindsay:

Houston International
Protocol Alliance
801 Congress, Suite 270
Houston, Texas 77002

The Earl of Lindsay*
Address
Country

Social Correspondence

The Earl and Countess of Lindsay
Address
Country

Place card

Lord Lindsay

Introductions: The Earl of Lindsay*

Conversation: Lord Lindsay

* This information applies to all three titles, substituting them where "earl" appears above. Some marquesses are entitled to the honorific "The Most Honorable"; others are not. Likewise, some earls and viscounts may be called "The Right Honorable," while for others this is not correct. In the United States, these honorifics are most often omitted altogether. They should never be included unless you are certain of the status of the individual.

Marchioness/Countess/Viscountess

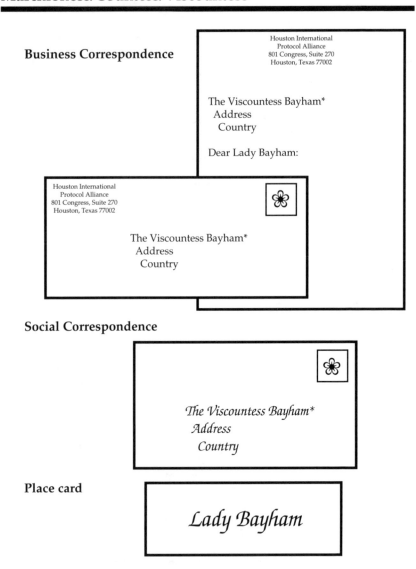

Business Correspondence

Houston International
Protocol Alliance
801 Congress, Suite 270
Houston, Texas 77002

The Viscountess Bayham*
Address
Country

Dear Lady Bayham:

Houston International
Protocol Alliance
801 Congress, Suite 270
Houston, Texas 77002

The Viscountess Bayham*
Address
Country

Social Correspondence

The Viscountess Bayham*
Address
Country

Place card

Lady Bayham

Introductions: The Viscountess Bayham

Conversation: Lady Bayham**

* This information applies to all three titles, substituting them where "viscountess"
appears above. See the footnote on the preceding page for information on the use of the
honorifics "The Most Honorable" and "The Right Honorable."
** Only an employee should call this individual "My Lady."

Business Correspondence

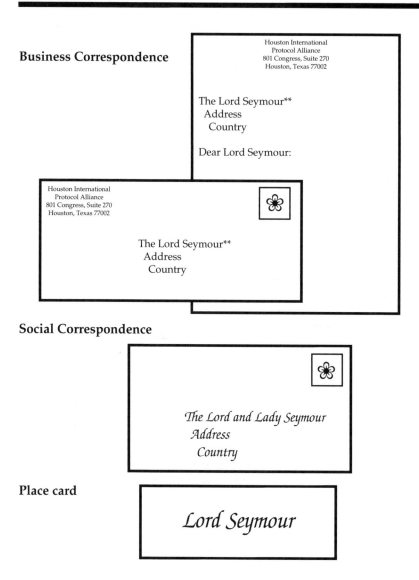

Houston International
Protocol Alliance
801 Congress, Suite 270
Houston, Texas 77002

The Lord Seymour**
Address
Country

Dear Lord Seymour:

Houston International
Protocol Alliance
801 Congress, Suite 270
Houston, Texas 77002

The Lord Seymour**
Address
Country

Social Correspondence

The Lord and Lady Seymour
Address
Country

Place card

Lord Seymour

Introductions: The Lord Seymour, The Lady Seymour

Conversation: Lord Seymour, Lady Seymour

* This information applies to British barons and their wives. Traditionally, the terms baron and baroness are not mentioned at all, unless it is necessary to do so for informational purposes.
**Some barons may be called "The Right Honorable"; others should not be. In the United States, we usually omit the honorific in all instances. Women who are baronesses in their own right may prefer to be called "The Right Honorable the Baroness Seymour" and could be addressed as "Baroness Seymour." However, the form above is most often used.

Baronet

Business Correspondence

Houston International
Protocol Alliance
801 Congress, Suite 270
Houston, Texas 77002

Sir George Wilson, Bt.*
Address
Country

Dear Sir George:

Houston International
Protocol Alliance
801 Congress, Suite 270
Houston, Texas 77002

Sir George Wilson, Bt.
Address
Country

Social Correspondence

*Sir George Wilson, Bt.
and Lady Wilson
Address
Country*

Place card

*Sir George Wilson***

Introductions: Sir George Wilson

Conversation: Sir George, Lady Wilson

* This title is nearly always abbreviated in writing, and is rarely used in introductions or conversation.
** His wife's place card would read "Lady Wilson."

Business Correspondence

Houston International
Protocol Alliance
801 Congress, Suite 270
Houston, Texas 77002

Sir George Wilson, G.C.B, K.C.M.G, C.B.*
Address
Country

Dear Sir George:

Houston International
Protocol Alliance
801 Congress, Suite 270
Houston, Texas 77002

❀

Sir George Wilson, G.C.B, K.C.M.G, C.B.*
Address
Country

Social Correspondence

❀

*Sir George Wilson, G.C.B, K.C.M.G, C.B.**
and Lady Wilson
Address
Country

Place card

Sir George Wilson

Introductions: Sir George Wilson

Conversation: Sir George, Lady Wilson

* Always include any initials that follow the individual's last name. They signify orders of knighthood or honors that the individual has received, and they follow a specific order. See page 86 for more information.

King*

Business Correspondence

Houston International
Protocol Alliance
801 Congress, Suite 270
Houston, Texas 77002

His Majesty
Bhumibol Adulyadej
King of Thailand
Address
City
Country

Your Majesty:

Houston International
Protocol Alliance
801 Congress, Suite 270
Houston, Texas 77002

His Majesty
Bhumibol Adulyadej
King of Thailand
Address
City
Country

Social Correspondence

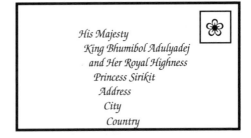

His Majesty
King Bhumibol Adulyadej
and Her Royal Highness
Princess Sirikit
Address
City
Country

Place card

His Majesty	*Her Royal Highness*
The King of Thailand	*Princess Sirikit*

Introductions: His Majesty, King Bhumibol Adulyadej of Thailand
Her Royal Highness, Princess Sirikit of Thailand

Conversation: Your Majesty and Your Royal Highness, or Sir and Ma'am

*Although similar to the information for the British Queen, this format applies to many nations around the world.

Business Correspondence

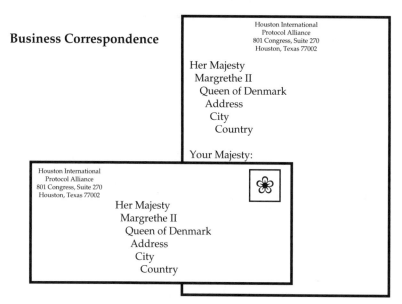

Houston International
Protocol Alliance
801 Congress, Suite 270
Houston, Texas 77002

Her Majesty
Margrethe II
Queen of Denmark
Address
City
Country

Your Majesty:

Houston International
Protocol Alliance
801 Congress, Suite 270
Houston, Texas 77002

Her Majesty
Margrethe II
Queen of Denmark
Address
City
Country

Social Correspondence

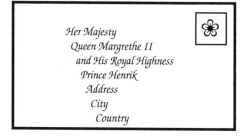

*Her Majesty
Queen Margrethe II
and His Royal Highness
Prince Henrik
Address
City
Country*

Place card

Her Majesty	*His Royal Highness*
The Queen of Denmark	*Prince Henrik*

Introductions: Her Majesty, Queen Margrethe II of Denmark
His Royal Highness, Prince Henrik of Denmark

Conversation: Your Majesty and Your Royal Highness

*This is a non-British example for a female reigning monarch.

King and Queen*

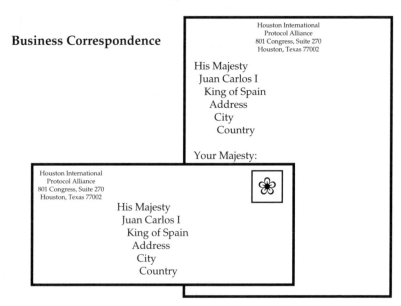

Business Correspondence

Houston International
Protocol Alliance
801 Congress, Suite 270
Houston, Texas 77002

His Majesty
Juan Carlos I
King of Spain
Address
City
Country

Your Majesty:

Houston International
Protocol Alliance
801 Congress, Suite 270
Houston, Texas 77002

His Majesty
Juan Carlos I
King of Spain
Address
City
Country

Social Correspondence

Their Majesties
The King and Queen of Spain
Address
City
Country

Place card

| *His Majesty* | *Her Majesty* |
| *The King of Spain* | *The Queen of Spain* |

Introductions: Their Majesties, the King and Queen of Spain

Conversation: Your Majesty, or Sir or Ma'am

* This entry is very similar to the British example earlier in this section.

Business Correspondence

Houston International
Protocol Alliance
801 Congress, Suite 270
Houston, Texas 77002

His Royal Highness
Abdullah ibn Abdul Aziz
Crown Prince of Saudi Arabia
Address
City
Country

Your Royal Highness:

Houston International
Protocol Alliance
801 Congress, Suite 270
Houston, Texas 77002

His Royal Highness
Abdullah ibn Abdul Aziz
Crown Prince of Saudi Arabia
Address
City
Country

Social Correspondence

His Royal Highness
Abdullah ibn Abdul Aziz
Crown Prince of Saudi Arabia
Address
City
Country

Place card

His Royal Highness
Crown Prince Abdullah

Introductions: His Royal Highness, Crown Prince Abdullah of Saudi Arabia

Conversation: Your Royal Highness, or Sir

Prince or Princess*

Business Correspondence

Houston International
Protocol Alliance
801 Congress, Suite 270
Houston, Texas 77002

Her Royal Highness
Princess Martha of Norway
Address
City
Country

Your Royal Highness:

Houston International
Protocol Alliance
801 Congress, Suite 270
Houston, Texas 77002

Her Royal Highness
Princess Martha of Norway
Address
City
Country

Social Correspondence

Her Royal Highness
Princess Martha of Norway
Address
City
Country

Place card

Her Royal Highness
Princess Martha

Introductions: Her Royal Highness, Princess Martha of Norway

Conversation: Your Royal Highness, or Ma'am

---

* Although a Norwegian example is used here, with slight modifications this form applies to other countries. For example, when addressing a Japanese prince, use "Imperial" instead of "Royal." For some individuals, only "His/Her Highness" is used.

Business Correspondence

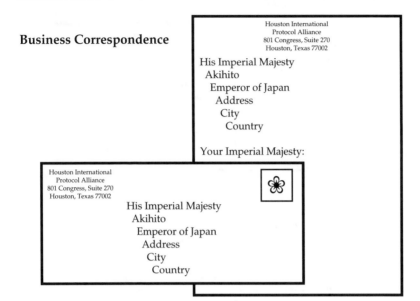

Houston International
Protocol Alliance
801 Congress, Suite 270
Houston, Texas 77002

His Imperial Majesty
Akihito
Emperor of Japan
Address
City
Country

Your Imperial Majesty:

Houston International
Protocol Alliance
801 Congress, Suite 270
Houston, Texas 77002

His Imperial Majesty
Akihito
Emperor of Japan
Address
City
Country

Social Correspondence

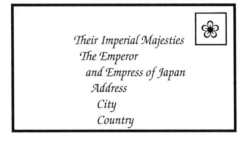

*Their Imperial Majesties
The Emperor
and Empress of Japan
Address
City
Country*

Place card

His Imperial Majesty *The Emperor of Japan*	*Her Imperial Majesty* *The Empress of Japan*

Introductions: His Imperial Majesty, the Emperor of Japan
Her Imperial Majesty, the Empress of Japan

Conversation: Your Imperial Majesty, or Sir or Ma'am

Business Correspondence

Houston International
Protocol Alliance
801 Congress, Suite 270
Houston, Texas 77002

His Serene Highness
Ranier III
Sovereign Prince of Monaco
Address
City
Country

Your Serene Highness:

Houston International
Protocol Alliance
801 Congress, Suite 270
Houston, Texas 77002

His Serene Highness
Ranier III
Sovereign Prince of Monaco
Address
City
Country

Social Correspondence

His Serene Highness
The Prince of Monaco
Address
City
Country

Place card

His Serene Highness
Ranier III

Introductions: His Serene Highness, Ranier III, Sovereign Prince of Monaco

Conversation: Your Serene Highness, or Prince Ranier

*Titles vary from country to country. Verify the correct form of address for each individual.

Business Correspondence

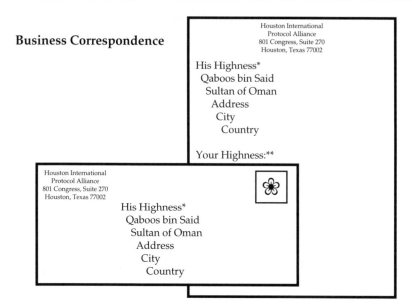

Houston International
Protocol Alliance
801 Congress, Suite 270
Houston, Texas 77002

His Highness*
Qaboos bin Said
Sultan of Oman
Address
City
Country

Your Highness:**

Houston International
Protocol Alliance
801 Congress, Suite 270
Houston, Texas 77002

His Highness*
Qaboos bin Said
Sultan of Oman
Address
City
Country

Social Correspondence

*Their Highnesses***
The Sultan
and Sultana of Oman
Address
City
Country

Place card

| *His Highness* | *Her Highness* |
| *The Sultan of Oman* | *The Sultana of Oman* |

Introductions: His Highness, Qaboos Bin Said, Sultan of Oman

Conversation: Your Highness, or Sir or Ma'am

* Honorifics vary from country to country. "His Royal Highness," "His Majesty," or some other variation may be correct in other cases.
** See note above.

Sheik*

Business Correspondence

Houston International
Protocol Alliance
801 Congress, Suite 270
Houston, Texas 77002

Sheik Mohammed Bin Abdul Al-Said**
Address
City
Country

Dear Sheik Al-Said:***

Houston International
Protocol Alliance
801 Congress, Suite 270
Houston, Texas 77002

Sheik Mohammed Bin Abdul Al-Said**
Address
City
Country

Social Correspondence

Sheik Mohammed Bin Abdul Al-Said
and Mrs. Al-Said
Address
City
Country

Place card

Sheik Al-Said

Introductions: Sheik Mohammed Bin Abdul Al-Said

Conversation: Sheik Al-Said

*Although included in this section, "sheik" is not considered to be a royal title and its significance varies from place to place. It sometimes denotes a tribal leader and it is sometimes used as a term of respect for a distinguished individual.

** This title is sometimes used with various honorifics, but we have omitted any here.

*** "Sheik Last Name" is perhaps most often used, but some places or individuals may prefer "Sheik First Name."

Religious Leaders

Each religious organization has its own hierarchy and customs that affect the way in which its officials are addressed. Although there are many more officials than can be included in this book, this section provides a basis for addressing various members of the clergy. When in doubt, always consult the individual or the religious authority as to their preferences.

Degrees

Many religious leaders hold advanced degrees that should be acknowledged. This is done by placing the initials appropriate for the degree after the full name: for example, "William Black, D.D., LL.D." (Doctor of Divinity, Doctor of Laws). In cases where the individual would otherwise be referred to as "Mr. Black," it is appropriate to use "Dr. Black." It is correct to use either "Dr." or the initials following the name, but never both at the same time. The degree initials are not used in social correspondence.

Honorifics

We have already noted that although most foreign government officials use "His Excellency" as the courtesy title of choice, all United States officials use "The Honorable." However, there are some Roman Catholic church officials in the United States who do use "His Excellency." They are bishops, archbishops, and apostolic delegates, and the proper forms of address for each are illustrated in this section. Honorifics for other religious officials are often unique.

Women

More and more women are taking leadership positions within religious organizations. The standard forms of address usually can be readily applied to female clergy members. We have illustrated the proper forms of address for a female Protestant minister as an example.

Religious Leaders

Islam

We are pleased to include forms of address for Islamic religious leaders. There are few standard references that contain this information, and because Islam is practiced in many countries around the world, usage varies. Furthermore, the translation of honorifics and titles from Arabic adds a layer of ambiguity. Arabic lends itself to more flowery forms of address than are typically used in English, and it seems that no exact English equivalents for certain terms have been widely adopted. Always follow the preferences of the individual or his mosque. We would appreciate hearing from any readers who can provide us with further information of interest with regard to Islamic forms of address.

Because Islam strongly influences the laws and customs of many nations, some political leaders may hold religious titles, and religious leaders hold political ones. In such cases, the preceding sections on royalty and foreign government officials may prove helpful.

Business Correspondence

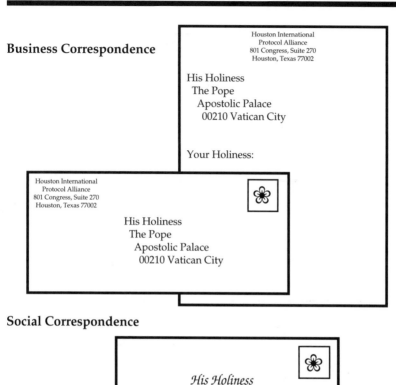

Houston International
Protocol Alliance
801 Congress, Suite 270
Houston, Texas 77002

His Holiness
The Pope
Apostolic Palace
00210 Vatican City

Your Holiness:

Houston International
Protocol Alliance
801 Congress, Suite 270
Houston, Texas 77002

His Holiness
The Pope
Apostolic Palace
00210 Vatican City

Social Correspondence

His Holiness
The Pope
Apostolic Palace
00210 Vatican City

Place card

His Holiness
The Pope

Introductions: His Holiness, the Pope

Conversation: Your Holiness

Roman Catholic Cardinal

Business Correspondence

> Houston International
> Protocol Alliance
> 801 Congress, Suite 270
> Houston, Texas 77002

His Eminence
Cardinal Wilson
Archbishop of Place*
Address
City, State Zip

Your Eminence:

> Houston International
> Protocol Alliance
> 801 Congress, Suite 270
> Houston, Texas 77002

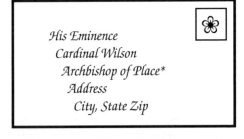

His Eminence
Cardinal Wilson
Archbishop of Place*
Address
City, State Zip

Social Correspondence

His Eminence
Cardinal Wilson
Archbishop of Place*
Address
City, State Zip

Place card

Cardinal Wilson

Introductions: His Eminence, Cardinal Wilson, Archbishop of Place*

Conversation: Your Eminence

*Cardinal is a personal distinction, not an office, and many cardinals hold the office of archbishop. Use the appropriate office title for the individual with whom you are corresponding.

Business Correspondence

Houston International
Protocol Alliance
801 Congress, Suite 270
Houston, Texas 77002

His Excellency
The Most Reverend
George Wilson
Archbishop of Place
The Apostolic Delegate
Washington, D.C.

Dear Archbishop:

Houston International
Protocol Alliance
801 Congress, Suite 270
Houston, Texas 77002

His Excellency
The Most Reverend
George Wilson
Archbishop of Place
The Apostolic Delegate
Washington, D.C.

Social Correspondence

His Excellency
The Most Reverend
George Wilson
Archbishop of Place
The Apostolic Delegate
Washington, D.C.

Place card

The Apostolic Delegate

Introductions: His Excellency the Most Reverend George Wilson, Archbishop of Place, the Apostolic Delegate

Conversation: Your Excellency, or Archbishop

Roman Catholic Archbishop

Business Correspondence

Houston International
Protocol Alliance
801 Congress, Suite 270
Houston, Texas 77002

His Excellency
The Most Reverend
George Wilson
Archbishop of Place
Address
City, State Zip

Dear Archbishop:

Houston International
Protocol Alliance
801 Congress, Suite 270
Houston, Texas 77002

His Excellency
The Most Reverend
George Wilson
Archbishop of Place
Address
City, State Zip

Social Correspondence

His Excellency
The Most Reverend
George Wilson
Archbishop of Place
Address
City, State Zip

Place card

Archbishop Wilson

Introductions: The Most Reverend George Wilson, Archbishop of Place, or His Excellency Archbishop Wilson

Conversation: Archbishop Wilson, or Your Excellency*

* In other countries, archbishops are often addressed as "Your Grace." In the United States and the United Kingdom, however, the above usage is preferred.

Business Correspondence

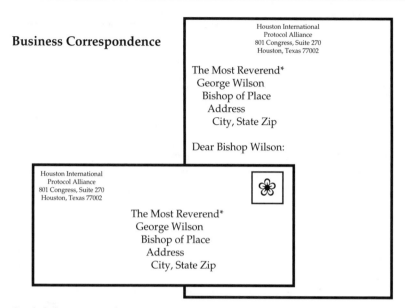

Houston International
Protocol Alliance
801 Congress, Suite 270
Houston, Texas 77002

The Most Reverend*
George Wilson
Bishop of Place
Address
City, State Zip

Dear Bishop Wilson:

Houston International
Protocol Alliance
801 Congress, Suite 270
Houston, Texas 77002

The Most Reverend*
George Wilson
Bishop of Place
Address
City, State Zip

Social Correspondence

The Most Reverend*
George Wilson
Bishop of Place
Address
City, State Zip

Place card

Bishop Wilson

Introductions: The Most Reverend George Wilson, Bishop of Place

Conversation: Bishop Wilson, or Bishop

---

*In some nations, bishops are referred to as "His Lordship" or "The Right Reverend." We have illustrated the United States usage.

Roman Catholic Priest

Business Correspondence

Houston International
Protocol Alliance
801 Congress, Suite 270
Houston, Texas 77002

The Reverend
George Wilson
Church Name
Address
City, State Zip

Dear Father Wilson:

Houston International
Protocol Alliance
801 Congress, Suite 270
Houston, Texas 77002

The Reverend
George Wilson
Church Name
Address
City, State Zip

Social Correspondence

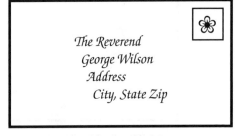

The Reverend
George Wilson
Address
City, State Zip

Place card

Father Wilson

Introductions: The Reverend George Wilson

Conversation: Father Wilson, or Father

Business Correspondence

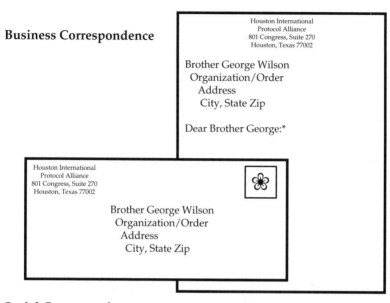

Houston International
Protocol Alliance
801 Congress, Suite 270
Houston, Texas 77002

Brother George Wilson
Organization/Order
Address
City, State Zip

Dear Brother George:*

Houston International
Protocol Alliance
801 Congress, Suite 270
Houston, Texas 77002

Brother George Wilson
Organization/Order
Address
City, State Zip

Social Correspondence

Brother George Wilson
Address
City, State Zip

Place card

Brother George Wilson

Introductions: Brother George Wilson

Conversation: Brother George, or Brother Wilson*

---

* For a sister, the individual's full name should be used at all times, even in salutations.

Episcopal Bishop

Business Correspondence

Houston International
Protocol Alliance
801 Congress, Suite 270
Houston, Texas 77002

The Right Reverend
George Wilson
Bishop of Houston
Address
City, State Zip

Dear Bishop Wilson:

Houston International
Protocol Alliance
801 Congress, Suite 270
Houston, Texas 77002

The Right Reverend
George Wilson
Bishop of Houston
Address
City, State Zip

Social Correspondence

The Right Reverend
George Wilson
and Mrs. Wilson
Address
City, State Zip

Place card

Bishop Wilson

Introductions: The Right Reverend George Wilson, Bishop of Houston

Conversation: Bishop Wilson, or Bishop*

148

* Outside of the United States, "My Lord" is often used in speaking to the holder of this office.

Business Correspondence

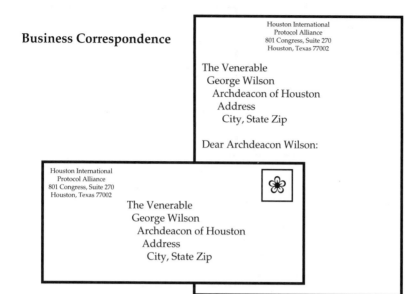

Houston International
Protocol Alliance
801 Congress, Suite 270
Houston, Texas 77002

The Venerable
George Wilson
Archdeacon of Houston
Address
City, State Zip

Dear Archdeacon Wilson:

Houston International
Protocol Alliance
801 Congress, Suite 270
Houston, Texas 77002

The Venerable
George Wilson
Archdeacon of Houston
Address
City, State Zip

Social Correspondence

The Venerable
George Wilson
and Mrs. Wilson
Address
City, State Zip

Place card

Archdeacon Wilson

Introductions: The Venerable George Wilson, Archdeacon of Houston

Conversation: Archdeacon Wilson, or Archdeacon

Episcopal Dean

Business Correspondence

Houston International
Protocol Alliance
801 Congress, Suite 270
Houston, Texas 77002

The Very Reverend
George Wilson
Dean of Church Name
Address
City, State Zip

Dear Dean Wilson:

Houston International
Protocol Alliance
801 Congress, Suite 270
Houston, Texas 77002

The Very Reverend
George Wilson
Dean of Church Name
Address
City, State Zip

Social Correspondence

The Very Reverend
George Wilson
and Mrs. Wilson
Address
City, State Zip

Place card

Dean Wilson

Introductions: The Very Reverend George Wilson, Dean of Church Name

Conversation: Dean Wilson, or Dean

Business Correspondence

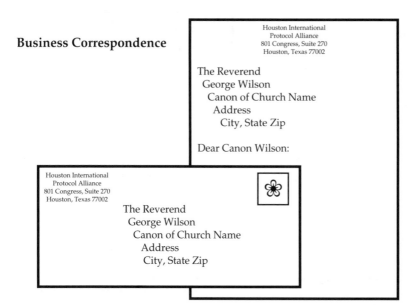

Houston International
Protocol Alliance
801 Congress, Suite 270
Houston, Texas 77002

The Reverend
George Wilson
Canon of Church Name
Address
City, State Zip

Dear Canon Wilson:

Houston International
Protocol Alliance
801 Congress, Suite 270
Houston, Texas 77002

The Reverend
George Wilson
Canon of Church Name
Address
City, State Zip

Social Correspondence

*The Reverend
George Wilson
and Mrs. Wilson
Address
City, State Zip*

Place card

Canon Wilson

Introductions: The Reverend George Wilson, Canon of Church Name

Conversation: Canon Wilson, or Canon

Business Correspondence

Houston International
Protocol Alliance
801 Congress, Suite 270
Houston, Texas 77002

His All Holiness
  Patriarch George
    Address
     City
      Country

Your All Holiness:

Houston International
Protocol Alliance
801 Congress, Suite 270
Houston, Texas 77002

His All Holiness
  Patriarch George
    Address
     City
      Country

Social Correspondence

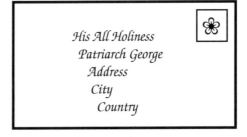

His All Holiness
Patriarch George
Address
City
Country

Place card

His All Holiness
Patriarch George

Introductions: His All Holiness, Patriarch George

Conversation: Your All Holiness

* Forms of address may differ for other orthodox churches. We have used the Greek Orthodox Church as our example because of its size in the United States.

Business Correspondence

Houston International
Protocol Alliance
801 Congress, Suite 270
Houston, Texas 77002

The Most Reverend
Archbishop George
Position Title
Address
City, State Zip

Your Eminence:

Houston International
Protocol Alliance
801 Congress, Suite 270
Houston, Texas 77002

The Most Reverend
Archbishop George
Position Title
Address
City, State Zip

Social Correspondence

The Most Reverend
Archbishop George
Address
City, State Zip

Place card

Archbishop George

Introductions: His Eminence Archbishop George of Position Title

Conversation: Your Eminence

* Forms of address may differ for other orthodox churches. We have used the Greek
Orthodox Church as our example because of its size in the United States.

Greek Orthodox Bishop*

Business Correspondence

Houston International
Protocol Alliance
801 Congress, Suite 270
Houston, Texas 77002

The Right Reverend George
Bishop of Place
Address
City, State Zip

Your Grace:

Houston International
Protocol Alliance
801 Congress, Suite 270
Houston, Texas 77002

The Right Reverend George
Bishop of Place
Address
City, State Zip

Social Correspondence

The Right Reverend George
Bishop of Place
Address
City, State Zip

Place card

Bishop George

Introductions: The Right Reverend George, Bishop of Place

Conversation: Your Grace, or Bishop George

---

* Forms of address may differ for other orthodox churches. We have used the Greek Orthodox Church as our example because of its size in the United States.

Greek Orthodox Archimandrite*

Business Correspondence

Houston International
Protocol Alliance
801 Congress, Suite 270
Houston, Texas 77002

The Very Reverend
George Wilson
Archimandrite
Address
City, State Zip

Dear Father Wilson:

Houston International
Protocol Alliance
801 Congress, Suite 270
Houston, Texas 77002

The Very Reverend
George Wilson
Archimandrite
Address
City, State Zip

Social Correspondence

*The Very Reverend
George Wilson
Address
City, State Zip*

Place card

Father George

Introductions: The Very Reverend George Wilson, Archimandrite

Conversation: Father George

---

* Forms of address may differ for other orthodox churches. We have used the Greek Orthodox Church as our example because of its size in the United States.

Business Correspondence

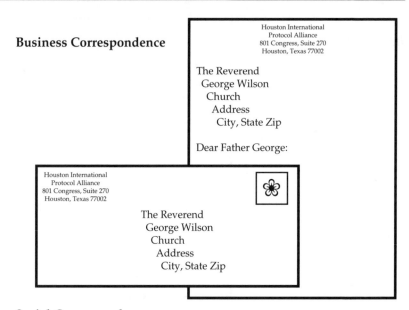

Houston International
Protocol Alliance
801 Congress, Suite 270
Houston, Texas 77002

The Reverend
George Wilson
Church
Address
City, State Zip

Dear Father George:

Houston International
Protocol Alliance
801 Congress, Suite 270
Houston, Texas 77002

The Reverend
George Wilson
Church
Address
City, State Zip

Social Correspondence

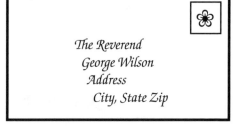

The Reverend
George Wilson
Address
City, State Zip

Place card

Father George

Introductions: The Reverend George Wilson

Conversation: Father George

* Forms of address may differ for other orthodox churches. We have used the Greek Orthodox Church as our example because of its size in the United States.

Business Correspondence

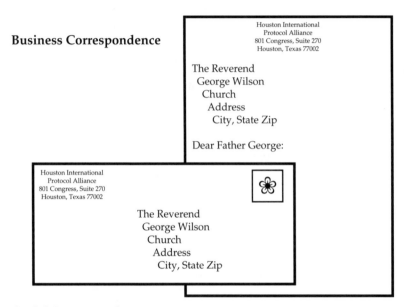

Houston International
Protocol Alliance
801 Congress, Suite 270
Houston, Texas 77002

The Reverend
George Wilson
Church
Address
City, State Zip

Dear Father George:

Houston International
Protocol Alliance
801 Congress, Suite 270
Houston, Texas 77002

The Reverend
George Wilson
Church
Address
City, State Zip

Social Correspondence

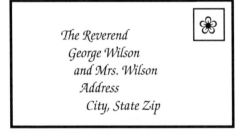

*The Reverend
George Wilson
and Mrs. Wilson
Address
City, State Zip*

Place card

Father George

Introductions: The Reverend George Wilson

Conversation: Father George

* Forms of address may differ for other orthodox churches. We have used the Greek Orthodox Church as our example because of its size in the United States.

Business Correspondence

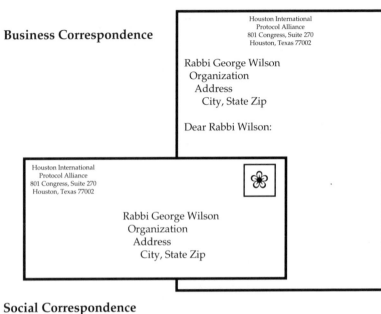

Houston International
Protocol Alliance
801 Congress, Suite 270
Houston, Texas 77002

Rabbi George Wilson
Organization
Address
City, State Zip

Dear Rabbi Wilson:

Houston International
Protocol Alliance
801 Congress, Suite 270
Houston, Texas 77002

Rabbi George Wilson
Organization
Address
City, State Zip

Social Correspondence

Rabbi and Mrs. George Wilson
Address
City, State Zip

Place card

Rabbi Wilson

Introductions: Rabbi George Wilson

Conversation: Rabbi Wilson

Business Correspondence

Houston International
Protocol Alliance
801 Congress, Suite 270
Houston, Texas 77002

Cantor George Wilson
Organization
Address
City, State Zip

Dear Cantor Wilson:

Houston International
Protocol Alliance
801 Congress, Suite 270
Houston, Texas 77002

Cantor George Wilson
Organization
Address
City, State Zip

Social Correspondence

Cantor and Mrs. George Wilson
Address
City, State Zip

Place card

Cantor Wilson

Introductions: Cantor George Wilson

Conversation: Cantor Wilson

Business Correspondence

Houston International
Protocol Alliance
801 Congress, Suite 270
Houston, Texas 77002

Mr. George Wilson
President
Church of Jesus Christ of Latter-Day Saints
Address
City, State Zip

Dear Mr. Wilson:*

Houston International
Protocol Alliance
801 Congress, Suite 270
Houston, Texas 77002

❀

Mr. George Wilson
President
Church of Jesus Christ of Latter-Day Saints
Address
City, State Zip

Social Correspondence

❀

Mr. and Mrs. George Wilson
Address
City, State Zip

Place card

*Mr. Wilson**

Introductions: Mr. George Wilson, President of the Church of Jesus Christ of Latter-Day Saints

Conversation: Mr. Wilson, or President Wilson

* "President Wilson" is an alternative to "Mr. Wilson" in the salutation and on the place card.

Business Correspondence

Houston International
Protocol Alliance
801 Congress, Suite 270
Houston, Texas 77002

Mr. George Wilson
   Church of Jesus Christ of Latter-Day Saints
   Address
   City, State Zip

Dear Mr. Wilson:

Houston International
Protocol Alliance
801 Congress, Suite 270
Houston, Texas 77002

❀

Mr. George Wilson
   Church of Jesus Christ of Latter-Day Saints
   Address
   City, State Zip

Social Correspondence

❀

Mr. and Mrs. George Wilson
Address
City, State Zip

Place card

Mr. Wilson

Introductions: Mr. George Wilson of the Church of Jesus Christ of Latter-Day Saints

Conversation: Mr. Wilson

Methodist Bishop

Business Correspondence

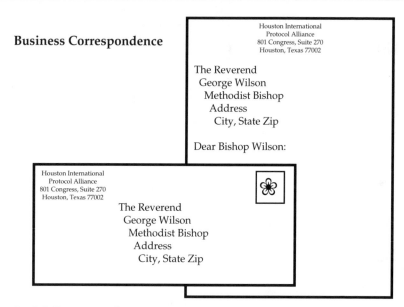

Houston International
Protocol Alliance
801 Congress, Suite 270
Houston, Texas 77002

The Reverend
George Wilson
Methodist Bishop
Address
City, State Zip

Dear Bishop Wilson:

Houston International
Protocol Alliance
801 Congress, Suite 270
Houston, Texas 77002

The Reverend
George Wilson
Methodist Bishop
Address
City, State Zip

Social Correspondence

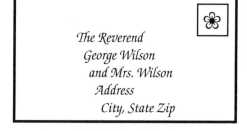

The Reverend
George Wilson
and Mrs. Wilson
Address
City, State Zip

Place card

Bishop Wilson

Introductions: The Reverend George Wilson, Bishop of Place of the
United Methodist Church

Conversation: Bishop Wilson

Business Correspondence

Houston International
Protocol Alliance
801 Congress, Suite 270
Houston, Texas 77002

The Reverend
George Wilson
Church
Address
City, State Zip

Dear Mr. Wilson:

Houston International
Protocol Alliance
801 Congress, Suite 270
Houston, Texas 77002

The Reverend
George Wilson
Church
Address
City, State Zip

Social Correspondence

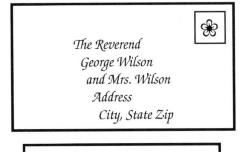

The Reverend
George Wilson
and Mrs. Wilson
Address
City, State Zip

Place card

Mr. Wilson

Introductions: The Reverend George Wilson of Church Name

Conversation: Mr. Wilson, or Pastor Wilson*

* Although commonly used, "Reverend Wilson" is not correct.

Female Minister (Protestant)*

Business Correspondence

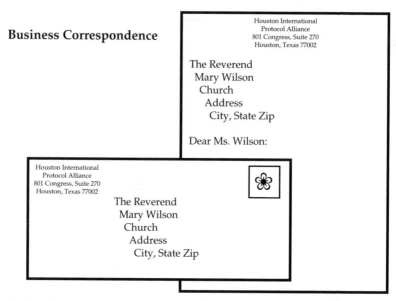

Houston International
Protocol Alliance
801 Congress, Suite 270
Houston, Texas 77002

The Reverend
Mary Wilson
Church
Address
City, State Zip

Dear Ms. Wilson:

Houston International
Protocol Alliance
801 Congress, Suite 270
Houston, Texas 77002

The Reverend
Mary Wilson
Church
Address
City, State Zip

Social Correspondence

The Reverend
Mary Wilson
and Mr. Wilson
Address
City, State Zip

Place card

Ms. Wilson

Introductions: The Reverend Mary Wilson of Church Name

Conversation: Ms. Wilson, or Minister Wilson**

---

* Forms of address for a female minister are essentially the same as for a male one.
** As previously noted, it would not be correct to say "Reverend Wilson."

Business Correspondence

Houston International
Protocol Alliance
801 Congress, Suite 270
Houston, Texas 77002

His Eminence
    Abdul Bin Yusuf Bin Khalid Al-Bassam
    The Grand Mufti of Jerusalem
    Address
    Country

Your Eminence:

Houston International
Protocol Alliance
801 Congress, Suite 270
Houston, Texas 77002

His Eminence
    Abdul Bin Yusuf Bin Khalid Al-Bassam
    The Grand Mufti of Jerusalem
    Address
    Country

Social Correspondence

His Eminence
The Grand Mufti of Jerusalem
Address
Country

Place card

The Grand Mufti
of Jerusalem

Introductions:	His Eminence the Grand Mufti of Jerusalem
Conversation:	Your Eminence

Imam (Islam)

Business Correspondence

Houston International
Protocol Alliance
801 Congress, Suite 270
Houston, Texas 77002

Imam Abdul Al-Rashid
Mosque Name
Address
City, State Zip

Dear Imam Al-Rashid:

Houston International
Protocol Alliance
801 Congress, Suite 270
Houston, Texas 77002

Imam Abdul Al-Rashid
Mosque Name
Address
City, State Zip

Social Correspondence

*Imam Abdul Al-Rashid
and Mrs. Al-Rashid
Mosque Name
Address
City, State Zip*

Place card

Imam Al-Rashid

Introductions: Abdul Al-Rashid, Imam of Mosque Name

Conversation: Imam Al-Rashid

Business Correspondence

Houston International
Protocol Alliance
801 Congress, Suite 270
Houston, Texas 77002

His Holiness
  Pope George III
    Pope of Alexandria
      Patriarch of the See of St. Mark
      Address
      Country

Your Holiness:

Houston International
Protocol Alliance
801 Congress, Suite 270
Houston, Texas 77002

His Holiness
  Pope George III
    Pope of Alexandria
      Patriarch of the See of St. Mark
      Address
      Country

Social Correspondence

His Holiness
  Pope George III
    Pope of Alexandria
      Patriarch of the See of St. Mark
      Address
      Country

Place card

His Holiness
Pope George III

Introductions: His Holiness Pope George III, Pope of Alexandria, Patriarch of the See of St. Mark

Conversation: Your Holiness

Dalai Lama (Buddhist)

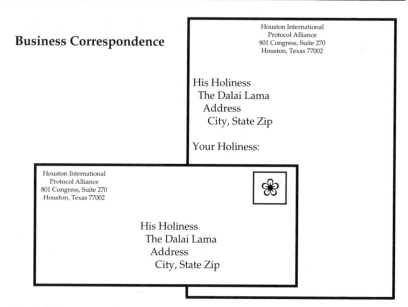

Business Correspondence

Houston International
Protocol Alliance
801 Congress, Suite 270
Houston, Texas 77002

His Holiness
The Dalai Lama
Address
City, State Zip

Your Holiness:

Houston International
Protocol Alliance
801 Congress, Suite 270
Houston, Texas 77002

His Holiness
The Dalai Lama
Address
City, State Zip

Social Correspondence

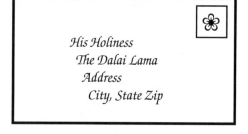

*His Holiness
The Dalai Lama
Address
City, State Zip*

Place card

*His Holiness
The Dalai Lama*

Introductions: His Holiness, the Dalai Lama

Conversation: Your Holiness

Archbishop of Canterbury or York (Church of England)

Business Correspondence

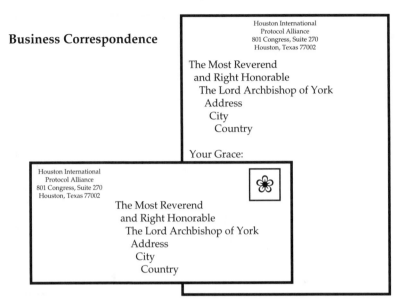

Houston International
Protocol Alliance
801 Congress, Suite 270
Houston, Texas 77002

The Most Reverend
and Right Honorable
The Lord Archbishop of York
Address
City
Country

Your Grace:

Houston International
Protocol Alliance
801 Congress, Suite 270
Houston, Texas 77002

The Most Reverend
and Right Honorable
The Lord Archbishop of York
Address
City
Country

Social Correspondence

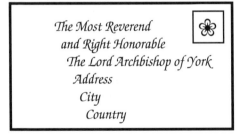

*The Most Reverend
and Right Honorable
The Lord Archbishop of York
Address
City
Country*

Place card

The Archbishop of York

Introductions: The Most Reverend and Right Honorable the Lord Archbishop of York

Conversation: Your Grace, or My Lord Archbishop

Chaplain (all service branches)

Business Correspondence

Houston International
Protocol Alliance
801 Congress, Suite 270
Houston, Texas 77002

Chaplain George Wilson
Captain, USAF
Address
City, State Zip

Dear Chaplain Wilson:

Houston International
Protocol Alliance
801 Congress, Suite 270
Houston, Texas 77002

Chaplain George Wilson
Captain, USAF
Address
City, State Zip

Social Correspondence

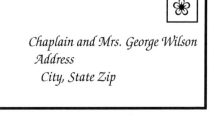

Chaplain and Mrs. George Wilson
Address
City, State Zip

Place card

Chaplain Wilson

Introductions: Chaplain Wilson

Conversation: Chaplain Wilson

United States Military

The following section explains the proper forms of address for members of the United States military. We have tried to simplify this information as much as possible by combining all service branches (where possible) and grades within each rank. Modify this information for each individual accordingly.

Women

The forms of address for female members of the armed forces are, as is the case for public officials, very similar to those used for their male counterparts. Socially, "Mr. and Mrs. John Smith" is always appropriate. To acknowledge the woman's title, however, the proper form is "General Mary P. Smith and Mr. John D. Smith." This differs from the social usage for other female officials only in that the husband's full name is used.

Rank

There are a few titles used in all service branches that have differing values between branches. For this reason, Army, Air Force, and Marine officials are treated separately here from those in the Navy and Coast Guard. For example, the title of captain is found in all service branches, but it is a much higher rank in the Navy and Coast Guard than it is elsewhere. The same is true for the rank of lieutenant.

Abbreviations

The use of abbreviations in formal correspondence should be avoided, particularly with regard to titles. Although names of the service branches are sometimes omitted entirely, they are often abbreviated in correspondence. When these abbreviations are used, they should follow the individual's last name and any degree initials that he or she uses. These are the most common abbreviations:

Army	USA	Navy	USN
Air Force	USAF	Marine Corps	USMC
Coast Guard	USCG		

Another abbreviation frequently used in correspondence with military officials is "Ret.," the designation for a retired officer. "Ret." follows the service branch designation and should be used only when space limitations disallow the use of the whole word. See page 185 for information on addressing retired officers.

Graded Titles

Titles that have several grades (for example, admiral, vice admiral, and rear admiral) are the most complex. In the Army, Air Force, and Marine Corps, the full title designation should be used only on envelopes and in formal introductions. Thus a brigadier general is simply "General" in salutations, in conversation, and on place cards. In the Navy and Coast Guard, the full rank is used on invitations and place cards as well as on envelopes.

Secretary of an Armed Service*

Business Correspondence

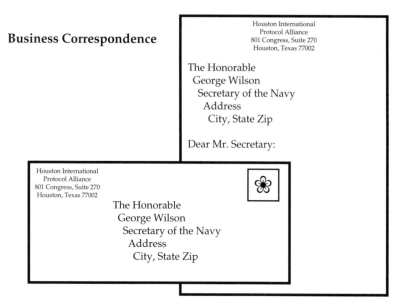

Houston International
Protocol Alliance
801 Congress, Suite 270
Houston, Texas 77002

The Honorable
George Wilson
   Secretary of the Navy
   Address
     City, State Zip

Dear Mr. Secretary:

Houston International
Protocol Alliance
801 Congress, Suite 270
Houston, Texas 77002

The Honorable
George Wilson
   Secretary of the Navy
   Address
     City, State Zip

Social Correspondence

The Honorable
The Secretary of the Navy
and Mrs. Wilson
Address
City, State Zip

Place card

The Secretary of the Navy

Introductions: The Honorable George Wilson, Secretary of the Navy

Conversation: Mr. Secretary, or Mr. Wilson

---

* Although this is not a cabinet-level post, the holder of this position is addressed just as a cabinet member is.

Under Secretary of an Armed Service

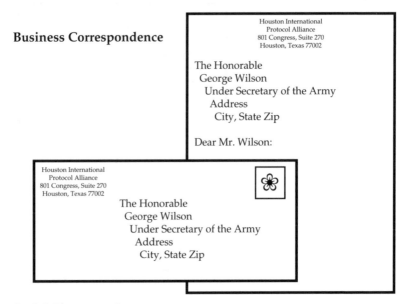

Business Correspondence

Houston International
Protocol Alliance
801 Congress, Suite 270
Houston, Texas 77002

The Honorable
George Wilson
    Under Secretary of the Army
    Address
    City, State Zip

Dear Mr. Wilson:

Houston International
Protocol Alliance
801 Congress, Suite 270
Houston, Texas 77002

The Honorable
George Wilson
    Under Secretary of the Army
    Address
    City, State Zip

Social Correspondence

The Honorable
The Under Secretary of the Army
and Mrs. Wilson
Address
City, State Zip

Place card

The Under Secretary
of the Army

Introductions: The Honorable George Wilson, Under Secretary of the Army

Conversation: Mr. Wilson

Business Correspondence

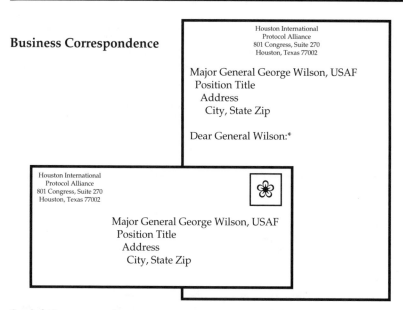

Houston International
Protocol Alliance
801 Congress, Suite 270
Houston, Texas 77002

Major General George Wilson, USAF
Position Title
Address
City, State Zip

Dear General Wilson:*

Houston International
Protocol Alliance
801 Congress, Suite 270
Houston, Texas 77002

Major General George Wilson, USAF
Position Title
Address
City, State Zip

Social Correspondence

Major General and Mrs. George Wilson
Address
City, State Zip

Place card

General Wilson *

Introductions: Major General George Wilson, Position Title

Conversation: General Wilson*

---

* This format is appropriate for lieutenant generals, major generals, and brigadier generals in the Army, Air Force, and Marine Corps. In salutations, on place cards, and in conversation, "General" is used for all these titles.

Captain/Major/Colonel/Lieutenant Colonel* **

Business Correspondence

Houston International
Protocol Alliance
801 Congress, Suite 270
Houston, Texas 77002

Major George Wilson, USA
Address
City, State Zip

Dear Major Wilson:

Houston International
Protocol Alliance
801 Congress, Suite 270
Houston, Texas 77002

Major George Wilson, USA
Address
City, State Zip

Social Correspondence

Major and Mrs. George Wilson
Address
City, State Zip

Place card

Major Wilson

Introductions: Major George Wilson

Conversation: Major Wilson, or Major

* For a lieutenant colonel, "Colonel Wilson" is used in the salutation and in conversation.

** This format is appropriate for these ranks in the Army, Air Force, and Marine Corps. Forms of address for Navy and Coast Guard officers appear later in this section.

Business Correspondence

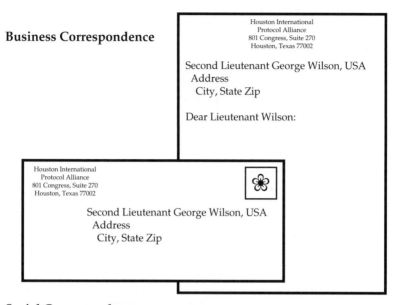

Houston International
Protocol Alliance
801 Congress, Suite 270
Houston, Texas 77002

Second Lieutenant George Wilson, USA
Address
City, State Zip

Dear Lieutenant Wilson:

Houston International
Protocol Alliance
801 Congress, Suite 270
Houston, Texas 77002

Second Lieutenant George Wilson, USA
Address
City, State Zip

Social Correspondence

Second Lieutenant and Mrs. George Wilson
Address
City, State Zip

Place card

Lieutenant Wilson

Introductions: Second Lieutenant George Wilson

Conversation: Lieutenant Wilson

---

* This format is appropriate for these ranks in the Army, Air Force, and Marine Corps.
Forms of address for Navy and Coast Guard officers appear later in this section.

Noncommissioned Officer*

Business Correspondence

Houston International
Protocol Alliance
801 Congress, Suite 270
Houston, Texas 77002

Sergeant Major George Wilson, USMC
Address
   City, State Zip

Dear Sergeant Wilson:

Houston International
Protocol Alliance
801 Congress, Suite 270
Houston, Texas 77002

❀

Sergeant Major George Wilson, USMC
Address
   City, State Zip

Social Correspondence

❀

Sergeant Major and Mrs. George Wilson
Address
   City, State Zip

Place card

Mr. Wilson

Introductions: Sergeant Major Wilson

Conversation: Sergeant Major Wilson

* This format is appropriate for all sergeants, corporals, specialists, airmen, and privates. Substitute titles as required.

Business Correspondence

Houston International
Protocol Alliance
801 Congress, Suite 270
Houston, Texas 77002

Vice Admiral George Wilson, USCG
Address
City, State Zip

Dear Admiral Wilson:**

Houston International
Protocol Alliance
801 Congress, Suite 270
Houston, Texas 77002

❀

Vice Admiral George Wilson, USCG
Address
City, State Zip

Social Correspondence

❀

Vice Admiral and Mrs. George Wilson
Address
City, State Zip

Place card

Vice Admiral Wilson

Introductions: Vice Admiral George Wilson, Position Title

Conversation: Admiral Wilson**

---

* This format is appropriate for all three ranks in the Navy as well as the Coast Guard.
** In the salutation and in conversation, "Admiral" is appropriate for all three ranks.

Commander/Captain/Commodore*

Business Correspondence

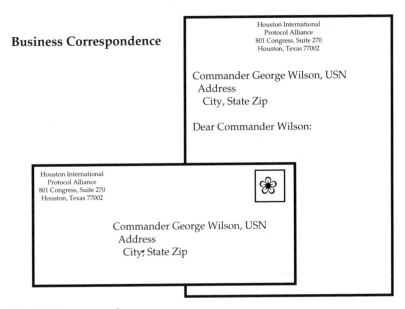

Houston International
Protocol Alliance
801 Congress, Suite 270
Houston, Texas 77002

Commander George Wilson, USN
Address
  City, State Zip

Dear Commander Wilson:

Houston International
Protocol Alliance
801 Congress, Suite 270
Houston, Texas 77002

Commander George Wilson, USN
Address
  City, State Zip

Social Correspondence

Commander and Mrs. George Wilson
Address
  City, State Zip

Place card

Commander Wilson

Introductions: Commander George Wilson

Conversation: Commander Wilson, or Commander

* This format is appropriate for all three ranks in the Navy as well as the Coast Guard.

Business Correspondence

Houston International
Protocol Alliance
801 Congress, Suite 270
Houston, Texas 77002

Lieutenant George Wilson, USN
Address
City, State Zip

Dear Mr. Wilson:

Houston International
Protocol Alliance
801 Congress, Suite 270
Houston, Texas 77002

Lieutenant George Wilson, USN
Address
City, State Zip

Social Correspondence

Lieutenant and Mrs. George Wilson
Address
City, State Zip

Place card

Lieutenant Wilson

Introductions: Lieutenant George Wilson

Conversation: Lieutenant Wilson, or Mr. Wilson

---

* This format is appropriate for the ranks of lieutenant commander; lieutenant; lieutenant, junior grade; and ensign in the Navy as well as the Coast Guard.

Noncommissioned Officer*

Business Correspondence

Houston International
Protocol Alliance
801 Congress, Suite 270
Houston, Texas 77002

Corporal George Wilson, USN
Address
City, State Zip

Dear Mr. Wilson:

Houston International
Protocol Alliance
801 Congress, Suite 270
Houston, Texas 77002

❀

Corporal George Wilson, USN
Address
City, State Zip

Social Correspondence

❀

Mr. and Mrs. George Wilson
Address
City, State Zip

Place card

Mr. Wilson

Introductions: Corporal George Wilson

Conversation: Mr. Wilson

* This format is appropriate for the Navy as well as the Coast Guard.

Business Correspondence

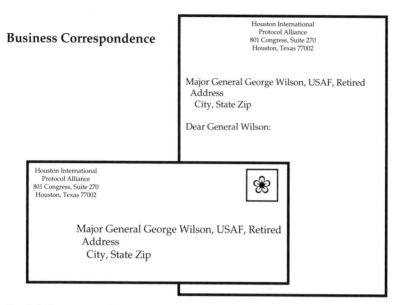

Houston International
Protocol Alliance
801 Congress, Suite 270
Houston, Texas 77002

Major General George Wilson, USAF, Retired
Address
City, State Zip

Dear General Wilson:

Houston International
Protocol Alliance
801 Congress, Suite 270
Houston, Texas 77002

❀

Major General George Wilson, USAF, Retired
Address
City, State Zip

Social Correspondence

❀

Major General and Mrs. George Wilson
Address
City, State Zip

Place card

General Wilson

Introductions: Major General George Wilson, USAF, Retired

Conversation: General Wilson

---

* These forms of address are not applicable to reserve officers, who do not retain their titles upon retirement.

Professionals, Academics,
and Other Private Citizens

Although particular complexities arise when addressing people with government rank or royal title, forms of address for private citizens also require special care. It is just as important to properly address a university president or a CEO as it is a king or an ambassador. In fact, the people with whom we are in most frequent contact are often most likely to expect us to address them correctly. As always, attention to detail is important. We hope that the examples in this section will serve as a guide to handling some common situations.

Professional Titles

Many individuals hold professional titles that affect the way in which they should be addressed. The following are just a few examples:

Doctorate Degree	Ph.D.
Medical Doctor	M.D.
Dentist	D.D.S.
Nurse	R.N.
Architect	A.I.A.
Designer	A.S.I.D.
Accountant	C.P.A.

To give full acknowledgment to the title, the initials should be placed after the last name: for example, "George Wilson, C.P.A." or "Mary Wilson, A.S.I.D." With this format, titles such as Mr., Ms., or Dr. should not be placed before the name. It is equally correct to use "Mr. George Wilson" or "Ms. Mary Wilson," but without the initials. We suggest basing your choice on the preferences of the individual. For example, some people with Ph.D. degrees prefer not to use their titles at all if they are not in a research or teaching position. Degree initials should not be used socially. Rather, use "Dr.," "Mr.," or "Ms." on personal letters and invitations.

Professionals, Academics, and Other Private Citizens

Foreign Titles

If you regularly correspond with people in other countries, it is likely that you will encounter professional titles such as "Dottore," "Ingeniero," or "Licenciado." Such titles are used much more frequently in other countries than they would be here in the United States. The exact degree equivalents for these titles vary from country to country, but if a foreign colleague uses one, be sure to use it in correspondence with him or her. We do not recommend trying to translate these titles; just use them as they are. In some countries, it is a sign of respect to call professionals by their titles, as in "Mr. Architect" or "Mrs. Director General," omitting names almost entirely.

Business Correspondence

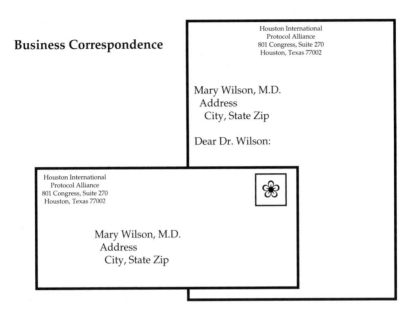

Houston International
Protocol Alliance
801 Congress, Suite 270
Houston, Texas 77002

Mary Wilson, M.D.
Address
City, State Zip

Dear Dr. Wilson:

Houston International
Protocol Alliance
801 Congress, Suite 270
Houston, Texas 77002

Mary Wilson, M.D.
Address
City, State Zip

Social Correspondence

Mr. George Wilson and Dr. Mary Wilson
Address
City, State Zip

Place card

Dr. Wilson

Introductions: Dr. Mary Wilson

Conversation: Dr. Wilson

Dentist

Business Correspondence

Houston International
Protocol Alliance
801 Congress, Suite 270
Houston, Texas 77002

George Wilson, D.D.S.
Address
   City, State Zip

Dear Dr. Wilson:

Houston International
Protocol Alliance
801 Congress, Suite 270
Houston, Texas 77002

❀

George Wilson, D.D.S.
Address
   City, State Zip

Social Correspondence

❀

Dr. and Mrs. George Wilson
Address
   City, State Zip

Place card

Dr. Wilson

Introductions: Dr. George Wilson

Conversation: Dr. Wilson

Business Correspondence

Houston International
Protocol Alliance
801 Congress, Suite 270
Houston, Texas 77002

Mary Wilson, R.N.
Address
City, State Zip

Dear Ms. Wilson:

Houston International
Protocol Alliance
801 Congress, Suite 270
Houston, Texas 77002

Mary Wilson, R.N.
Address
City, State Zip

Social Correspondence

*Ms. Mary Wilson
and Guest
Address
City, State Zip*

Place card

Ms. Wilson

Introductions: Ms. Mary Wilson

Conversation: Ms. Wilson

Veterinarian

Business Correspondence

Houston International
Protocol Alliance
801 Congress, Suite 270
Houston, Texas 77002

George Wilson, D.V.M.
Address
City, State Zip

Dear Dr. Wilson:

Houston International
Protocol Alliance
801 Congress, Suite 270
Houston, Texas 77002

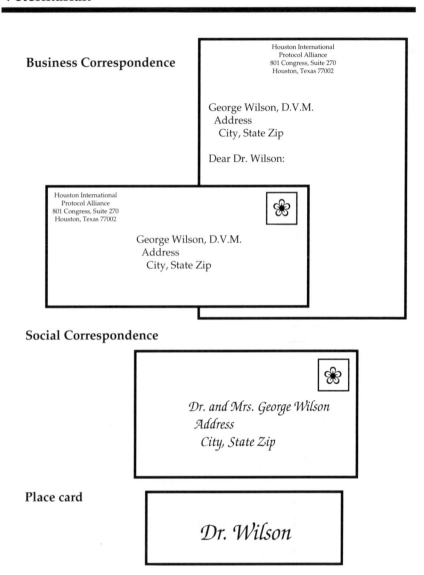

George Wilson, D.V.M.
Address
City, State Zip

Social Correspondence

Dr. and Mrs. George Wilson
Address
City, State Zip

Place card

Dr. Wilson

Introductions: Dr. George Wilson

Conversation: Dr. Wilson

Business Correspondence

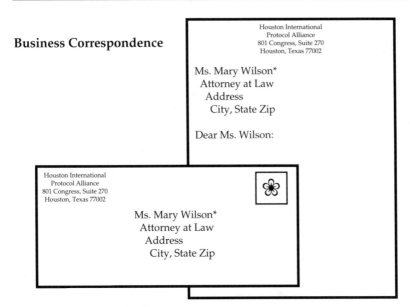

Houston International
Protocol Alliance
801 Congress, Suite 270
Houston, Texas 77002

Ms. Mary Wilson*
Attorney at Law
Address
City, State Zip

Dear Ms. Wilson:

Houston International
Protocol Alliance
801 Congress, Suite 270
Houston, Texas 77002

Ms. Mary Wilson*
Attorney at Law
Address
City, State Zip

Social Correspondence

Mr. and Mrs. George Wilson
Address
City, State Zip

Place card

Ms. Wilson

Introductions: Ms. Mary Wilson

Conversation: Ms. Wilson

* Although "Mary Wilson, Esq." is still sometimes used, the title seems to be well on its way to extinction, and we prefer to omit it.

Business Correspondence

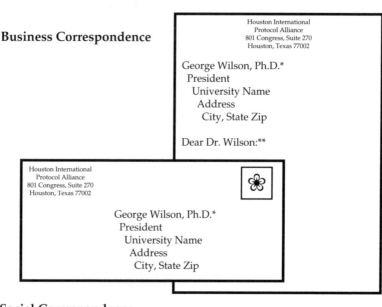

Houston International
Protocol Alliance
801 Congress, Suite 270
Houston, Texas 77002

George Wilson, Ph.D.*
President
University Name
Address
City, State Zip

Dear Dr. Wilson:**

Houston International
Protocol Alliance
801 Congress, Suite 270
Houston, Texas 77002

George Wilson, Ph.D.*
President
University Name
Address
City, State Zip

Social Correspondence

Dr. and Mrs. George Wilson
Address
City, State Zip

Place card

Dr. Wilson

Introductions: Dr. George Wilson, President of University Name

Conversation: Dr. Wilson, or President Wilson

---

* Use whatever degree initials apply to the individual.

196 ** Substituting "President Wilson" for "Dr. Wilson" would also be appropriate.

Business Correspondence

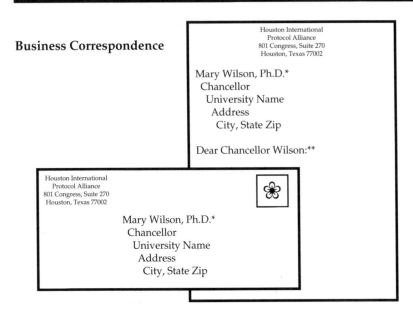

Houston International
Protocol Alliance
801 Congress, Suite 270
Houston, Texas 77002

Mary Wilson, Ph.D.*
Chancellor
University Name
Address
City, State Zip

Dear Chancellor Wilson:**

Houston International
Protocol Alliance
801 Congress, Suite 270
Houston, Texas 77002

Mary Wilson, Ph.D.*
Chancellor
University Name
Address
City, State Zip

Social Correspondence

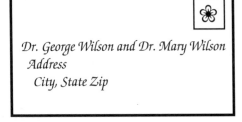

Dr. George Wilson and Dr. Mary Wilson
Address
City, State Zip

Place card

*Chancellor Wilson***

Introductions: Dr. Mary Wilson, Chancellor of University Name

Conversation: Chancellor Wilson, or Dr. Wilson

* Use whatever degree initials are appropriate for the individual.
** "Dr. Wilson" would also be appropriate.

Dean of a College or University

Business Correspondence

George Wilson, Ph.D.*
   Dean of the School of Subject Name
   University Name
   Address
     City, State Zip

Dear Dr. Wilson:**

George Wilson, Ph.D.*
   Dean of the School of Subject Name
   University Name
   Address
     City, State Zip

Social Correspondence

Dr. and Mrs. George Wilson
Address
City, State Zip

Place card

*Dr. Wilson***

Introductions: Dr. George Wilson, Dean of the School of Subject
Name at University Name

Conversation: Dr. Wilson, or Dean Wilson

---

* Use whatever degree initials are appropriate for the individual.
** "Dean Wilson" would also be appropriate.

Professor/Assistant Professor/Associate Professor*

Business Correspondence

Houston International
Protocol Alliance
801 Congress, Suite 270
Houston, Texas 77002

George Wilson, Ph.D.**
Associate Professor
University Name
Address
City, State Zip

Dear Dr. Wilson:***

Houston International
Protocol Alliance
801 Congress, Suite 270
Houston, Texas 77002

❀

George Wilson, Ph.D.**
Associate Professor
University Name
Address
City, State Zip

Social Correspondence

❀

Dr. and Mrs. George Wilson
Address
City, State Zip

Place card

*Dr. Wilson****

Introductions: Dr. George Wilson

Conversation: Dr. Wilson, or Professor Wilson

* This information applies to all three titles by substituting the appropriate title where indicated.
** Use any degree initials that apply to the individual. "Professor George Wilson" could also be used here, without degree initials.
*** "Professor Wilson" could be substituted here.

President of a Hospital

Business Correspondence

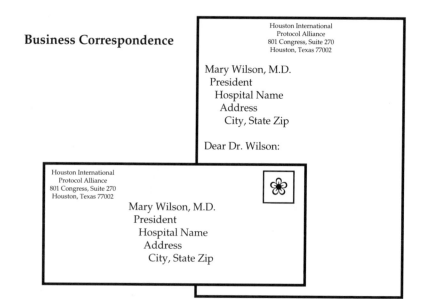

Houston International
Protocol Alliance
801 Congress, Suite 270
Houston, Texas 77002

Mary Wilson, M.D.
President
Hospital Name
Address
City, State Zip

Dear Dr. Wilson:

Houston International
Protocol Alliance
801 Congress, Suite 270
Houston, Texas 77002

Mary Wilson, M.D.
President
Hospital Name
Address
City, State Zip

Social Correspondence

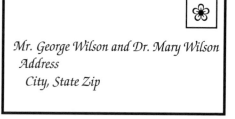

Mr. George Wilson and Dr. Mary Wilson
Address
City, State Zip

Place card

Dr. Wilson

Introductions: Dr. Mary Wilson

Conversation: Dr. Wilson

Business Correspondence

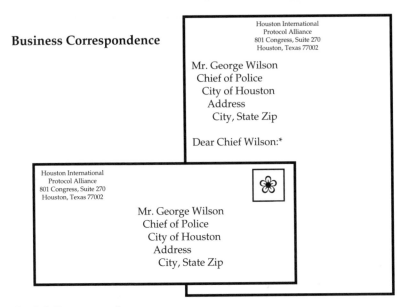

Houston International
Protocol Alliance
801 Congress, Suite 270
Houston, Texas 77002

Mr. George Wilson
Chief of Police
City of Houston
Address
City, State Zip

Dear Chief Wilson:*

Houston International
Protocol Alliance
801 Congress, Suite 270
Houston, Texas 77002

Mr. George Wilson
Chief of Police
City of Houston
Address
City, State Zip

Social Correspondence

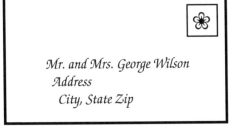

Mr. and Mrs. George Wilson
Address
City, State Zip

Place card

*Chief Wilson**

Introductions: Mr. George Wilson, Chief of Police

Conversation: Chief Wilson, or Mr. Wilson

* "Mr. Wilson" would also be appropriate.

Chief Executive Officer*

Business Correspondence

Houston International
Protocol Alliance
801 Congress, Suite 270
Houston, Texas 77002

Ms. Mary Wilson
  Chief Executive Officer**
   Company Name
    Address
     City, State Zip

Dear Ms. Wilson:

Houston International
Protocol Alliance
801 Congress, Suite 270
Houston, Texas 77002

Ms. Mary Wilson
  Chief Executive Officer**
   Company Name
    Address
     City, State Zip

Social Correspondence

Mr. and Mrs. George Wilson
Address
City, State Zip

Place card

Ms. Wilson

Introductions: Ms. Mary Wilson

Conversation: Ms. Wilson

---

* This format also applies to other business titles: for example, chairman of the board, chief operating officer, and president.
** Use the individual's full title: for example, "President and Chief Executive Officer."

The information in this book has been accumulated through many years of research and practice at the Houston International Protocol Alliance. We have relied especially on the following books for guidance:

Baldrige, Letitia. *Letitia Baldrige's New Complete Guide to Executive Manners.* New York: Rawson Associates, MacMillan Publishing, 1993.

Innis, Pauline, and Walter D. Innis. *Attention! A Quick Guide to the Armed Services.* Washington, D.C.: Devon Publishing, 1988.

McCaffree, Mary Jane, and Pauline Innis. *Protocol: The Complete Handbook of Diplomatic, Official, and Social Use.* Washington, D.C.: Devon Publishing, 1985.

Morris, Allen. *Practical Protocol for Floridians.* Rev. 4th ed. Florida House of Representatives, 1988.

Post, Elizabeth L. *Emily Post's Etiquette.* Rev. 14th ed. New York: Harper and Row, 1984.

You may also find the following books helpful:

The Consular Corps of Houston. Quarterly directory published by the Houston International Protocol Alliance.

The Diplomatic List. Department of State Publication 7894, Government Printing Office, Washington, D.C.

Lawler, Rick. *How to Write to World Leaders.* New York: Avon Books, 1992.

Montague-Smith, Patrick, ed. *Debrett's Correct Form.* New York: Arco Publishing Company, Inc., 1977.

Titles and Forms of Address: A Guide to Correct Use. 19th ed. London: A & C Black (Publishers), 1990.

Index

A

B

Index

Index

F

Federal Government 27–52. *See also* United States
Female Officials 20
First Lady 30, 32
First Lieutenant 179
Foreign Government Officials 85

G

General 177
Governor 56
   elect 58
   foreign 100
   former 57
   rank of 55
Grand Mufti (Islam) 165
Greek Orthodox Church 152–157

H

Harris County, Texas 71
Head of Post 24
   honorary 106
Her Excellency 85
His Excellency
   for foreign officials 85
   in Roman Catholic Church 139
   for state officials 55
Hispanic names 88
Honorable, The 29, 55
   for foreign officials 85
   for judges 71
   for local officials 71
Honorary Consul 24, 106
Honorifics
   abbreviation of 17
   of foreign officials 85
   of religious leaders 139
House of Representatives
   Majority/Minority Leader of 46

Index

Index